conducting a job interview

MINUTE

10

GUIDE

Macmillan USA, Inc.
201 West 103rd Street
Indianapolis, IN 46290

A Pearson Education Company

Dr. William W. Larson

YO-BSS-558

10 Minute Guide to Conducting a Job Interview

International Standard Book Number: 0-02-863996-0
Library of Congress Catalog Card Number: Available upon request.

03   02   01   8   7   6   5   4   3   2   1

Interpretation of the printing code: The rightmost number of the first series of numbers is the year of the book's printing; the rightmost number of the second series of numbers is the number of the book's printing. For example, a printing code of 01-1 shows that the first printing occurred in 2001.

Printed in the United States of America

Note: This publication contains the opinions and ideas of its author. It is intended to provide helpful and informative material on the subject matter covered. It is sold with the understanding that the author and publisher are not engaged in rendering professional services in the book. If the reader requires personal assistance or advice, a competent professional should be consulted.

Dedicated to

Walter Howard Larson

Father, friend, and mentor

In loving memory

Contents

Introduction

In his biography, Lee Iacocca said, "I learned to figure people out pretty quickly. That's an important skill to have, because the most important thing any manager can do is hire the right new people."

If you're a manager charged with the responsibility of hiring new people for your organization, you need to recognize two things immediately: First, it is critical to the future of your organization that you hire only top-quality people who can hit the ground running and quickly contribute to the success of your enterprise. Second, the traditional hiring methods used by business and industry over the past 50 years don't work—you need to find better ways of separating potentially successful job candidates from also-rans.

The future of your organization is literally in your hands. Every time you hire a new employee you change the character and potential of your organization for better or worse. A uniquely wonderful opportunity belongs to those who conduct job interviews.

But there's also a downside. Hiring mistakes can be costly. Not only does this involve the direct cost of salary and benefits paid to an employee who fails, but it also includes the cost of filling and refilling the position. Some studies have shown that direct costs attributable to a hiring mistake can easily equal four times the annual salary allocated for the position—and that number increases appreciably if the mistake is not rectified within the first six months of employment.

Indirect costs can also be staggering. Lost productivity, damage to customer relations, drain on management, and the harm to employee morale also represent significant cost and can have long-term impact on the organization.

It's sad, but true, that in spite of the costs involved, most businesses today spend more time buying a new copy machine than they do choosing the right employee. The results are predictably disastrous.

In this age of corporate downsizing, when more is expected of a shrinking number of employees, the skill of identifying potentially successful candidates for employment is becoming an essential management skill. Hiring mistakes must be minimized by better-quality interviews that spot potential problems before financial commitments are made.

It's a fact: Exceptional managers are exceptional interviewers. They hire successful candidates who produce more, do more to help the organization outperform the competition, promote higher levels of employee morale, and overall make a significant contribution to bottom-line profitability.

And here's some good news: Becoming an exceptional interviewer isn't that difficult. Any manager who is willing to lay aside old interviewing habits and techniques, and replace them with the behaviorally based interviewing skills taught in this book, will soon become a truly exceptional interviewer.

Equipping busy managers to plan, conduct, and evaluate exceptional interviews is what this book is all about. My aim is to give managers the tools they need to evaluate job applicants and reveal real strengths and weaknesses that will directly impact that individual's ability to succeed on the job.

CONVENTIONS USED IN THIS BOOK

Scattered throughout the *10 Minute Guide to Conducting a Job Interview* are three icon boxes that contain useful and interesting additional information:

 TIP

> Tip boxes contain valuable suggestions to get you thinking.

PLAIN ENGLISH

> Plain English boxes define terms that might be new to you.

CAUTION

> Caution boxes advise you of potentially tricky or dangerous pitfalls.

THE AUTHOR

William W. Larson is a former Lutheran clergyman who holds a doctorate in management. He has served as the executive director and chief operating officer of Simon Greenleaf School of Law, and the executive director of the World Confessional Lutheran Association. He also is the founder and president of Selection Dynamics Institute of Tacoma, Washington, offering personalized training to supervisors and managers who make critical hiring decisions for their companies.

ACKNOWLEDGMENTS

I wish to thank everyone at Macmillan USA who helped make this book possible. I am particularly grateful to Publisher Marie Butler-Knight; Mike Sanders, Acquisitions Editor; Mike Thomas, Development Editor; Krista Hansing, Copy Editor; Billy Fields, Production Editor; and all those involved in the printing, sales, and distribution of this book. The Macmillan team has been professional, motivating, and simply wonderful to work with. Special thanks also to Mike Magno of Clover Park Technical College in Lakewood, Washington for acting as technical editor for this book.

TRADEMARKS

All terms mentioned in this book that are known to be or are suspected of being trademarks or service marks have been appropriately capitalized. Macmillan USA, Inc., cannot attest to the accuracy of this information. Use of a term in this book should not be regarded as affecting the validity of any trademark or service mark.

LESSON 1
Analyzing the Position

In this lesson, you learn the importance of beginning at the beginning—with the job itself! You learn how to analyze a job to uncover what's necessary for an employee to succeed and how to reveal a profile of the candidate you seek.

BEGINNING AT THE BEGINNING

Beginning at the beginning is always the sensible thing to do. That's especially true when it comes to conducting employment interviews. But just where does the road to a successful job interview begin? The answer: with the job itself!

Begin by embarking on a systematic review of the job, a process known as introspective investigation. Your objective is to collect as much information as possible about how the job is done and what knowledge and skills are needed to perform it. Here are a few suggestions that will help you collect the information you need:

- Take a close look at the official job description, paying particular attention to established performance standards.

- Consider the environment in which the job is performed. Are there any special skills required? For example, a public relations or sales position will usually be performed in an environment requiring exceptional interpersonal skills and an ability to relate to people with diverse interests.

- Determine the product produced by the job and what is required to ensure consistent quality of that product.

- Examine business plans that may affect the position. Will the job change as a result of changes in business strategy? A few years ago a friend of mine was hired as west coast field sales manager by a large national insurance company. In six months he was asked to relocate to the home office located in the Midwest. The company was implementing a portion of its business plan that changed the way in which its products would be sold. Direct marketing would replace field sales. The business plan had been developed prior to the time my friend was hired, but no one bothered to inform him of the impending changes.

- Make note of any machines or tools that must be used to perform the tasks of the job.

- Solicit the input of the person who supervises the position.

- Talk with workers in the organization who regularly interact with the position to determine their perspective on what qualifications the successful applicant should possess.

- Don't forget to talk with those who have held the job in the past. What competencies and skills contributed to their success? Did the lack of certain competencies or skills cause or contribute to difficulties that they experienced on the job?

Through *introspective investigation*, you gather the information that you need to begin the hiring process. There are no shortcuts, but if you're serious about matching the right job with the right candidate, time invested in this task will be well rewarded.

PLAIN ENGLISH

Introspective investigation   The process by which an organization examines the position to be filled. The goal of introspective investigation is to identify essential competencies, skills, and abilities required for successful performance of the job.

ANALYZING THE POSITION

The objective of introspective investigation is to discover what skills and competencies are necessary for successful performance of the job. When you've identified these skills and competencies, organize them into the following categories: technical competencies, functional skills, self-management skills, interpersonal skills, and requirements of the corporate culture.

TECHNICAL COMPETENCIES

Technical competencies include any certifications, degrees, licenses, experience, and so on required to do the job. For example, an accountant position may require a degree in business as well as certification by a recognized board of accountancy. The job of personnel manager may require a human resources degree and experience in union/management affairs. Technical competencies are sometimes prescribed by law (as in the case of physicians, nurses, psychologists, teachers, lawyers, and so on).

What technical competencies, if any, are required to perform the job?

 TIP

> Don't be concerned about prioritizing the competencies and skills you've included in your list. The initial task is to list them; we'll prioritize them later.

FUNCTIONAL SKILLS

Functional skills are skills that help people function effectively on the job. To help identify functional skills, complete this sentence: "The primary responsibilities of the job include _____, _____, _____, and _____." List each functional skill that is required to do the job.

Here are some examples of common functional skills:

- Communication (written and verbal)
- Management
- Analysis
- Supervision
- Leadership
- Delegation
- Listening ability
- Independence
- Entrepreneurial approach
- Safety consciousness
- Risk taking
- Detail orientation
- Judgment
- Initiative
- Development of subordinates
- Service orientation
- Resilience
- Flexibility
- Adaptability
- Innovation
- Negotiation
- Sensitivity
- Planning and organizing ability
- Training
- Mentoring
- Sales ability
- Stress management ability
- Public relations ability
- Teamwork
- Equipment operation

The functional skills required for success in a typical organization vary widely depending on the job. For example, to be successful, a sales associate position may require someone with above average communication skills (both written and verbal) as well as highly developed time-management skills.

Functional skills are skills that can be learned. In fact, the acquisition of functional skills is usually an important goal of ongoing corporate training programs and postgraduate continuing education.

Functional skills are also transferable. *Transferable* means that an individual who has demonstrated specific functional skills in other employment or life situations can apply the same skills to the challenges of a new situation.

What functional skills distinguish top performers in the position under consideration? Remember to list them all, regardless of the degree of importance.

SELF-MANAGEMENT SKILLS

Self-management skills are personal characteristics that enhance one's ability to do the job. In this category, you'll want to include such characteristics as these:

- Creativity
- Dependability
- Ethics
- Honesty
- Loyalty
- Reliability
- Tactfulness

- Appearance
- Competence
- Helpfulness
- Popularity
- Accountability
- Self-sufficiency

Unlike functional skills, self-management skills are acquired over a period of time and often have their roots in childhood. Although it is possible for someone to alter personal characteristics, change in this area is often difficult and complex, usually requiring the assistance of a professional counselor.

Self-management skills are an important part of the overall hiring equation. Concentrating on functional skills and neglecting to consider the personal characteristics of the applicant is a recipe for failure. Avoid it.

List each of the self-management skills that the ideal candidate should possess. Consider asking others for suggestions.

Interpersonal Skills

Interpersonal skills are "people skills." How people get along with each other, including how they communicate, is an important concern of any organization.

Good interpersonal skills include the ability to respect others, to be empathetic and caring, to listen attentively and respond accordingly, to maintain objectivity and refrain from emotionalism, and to communicate accurately and appropriately. These skills are rooted in a healthy understanding of oneself and others.

People with good interpersonal skills enjoy interacting with others. They recognize conflict to be a natural, normal, and sometimes even delightful part of life and are always prepared to explore ways to resolve conflict and reconcile differences.

Interpersonal skills help in any position. For some jobs, however, strong interpersonal skills are absolutely essential to success. For example, the success of a bean counter working in an obscure part of the office who rarely sees people will not be influenced much by his or her interpersonal skills. But the job of a sales and marketing executive who is responsible for conveying a positive company image as well as selling its products requires extraordinary interpersonal skills.

Consider the importance of interpersonal skills in the position under consideration. List any specific interpersonal skills that you feel apply to the position.

Requirements of the Corporate Culture

What additional requirements (written or otherwise) are imposed on the position by the culture in which it exists? Every organization has a unique culture that must be considered.

For example, it is the unwritten rule of some organizations that executives should always wear suits and ties (some organizations even prescribe the color of the suit!). In other organizations, it is expected that employees, regardless of where they are on the corporate ladder, always be involved in continuing education, or that they regularly participate in extracurricular company activities, or that they volunteer for various community projects and endeavors.

As ridiculous as cultural expectations may seem, the fact is that success within the culture is dependent upon compliance with that culture. Like it or not, that's the way it is. The organizational culture is sacred, and you must take it into account when hiring a new employee.

List any cultural expectations of your organization that you need to consider when interviewing candidates for the job.

 CAUTION

> Don't underestimate the demands that corporate culture places on employees. A new employee cannot succeed with your organization unless there's a good fit with the existing culture.

MANDATORY SUCCESS FACTORS

Each of the competencies and skills that you've discovered through introspective investigation, and that you've listed under the categories outlined previously, is important. Together they provide a profile of the job as well as the ideal candidate.

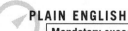 **PLAIN ENGLISH**

> **Mandatory success factors**   Those specific competencies and skills that are absolutely essential to successful job performance. They are determined through a process of introspective investigation and provide a profile of the job as well as the ideal candidate.

However, in preparing for the interview process, it's helpful to narrow the focus to those specific competencies and skills that are absolutely necessary to the successful performance of the job. From your list of skills and competencies, select each factor that is an absolute must. These are the position's mandatory success factors, and they will form the foundation for the process of interviewing and selecting.

In selecting the position's mandatory success factors, consider each of the categories listed above. Remember: these are the factors that are required for success in the position and are, therefore, the attributes that you'll want in your candidate of choice.

TIP

Ask two or three others familiar with the position to help you select the mandatory success factors. These may be the same individuals who will comprise your interview team.

CAUTION

Don't allow yourself to be rushed through the process of introspective investigation. Take the time that you need to find out just what is required for a new employee to succeed. This step alone will significantly increase your chance of hiring someone who will succeed. It's better to have an open position than to hire the wrong person for the job.

THE 30-SECOND RECAP

- Begin with a thorough analysis of the job.

- List each skill and competency even remotely associated with the job.

- From the list of skills and competencies, choose those factors that are absolutely essential to successful job performance.

LESSON 2
The Resumé

In this lesson, you learn how to use a resumé to select candidates to interview.

BEGINNING THE SELECTION PROCESS

There's a job opening in your organization. You're responsible for hiring the right person—someone who will succeed in the job and remain with the organization for the long term.

You've done your homework. You've identified the mandatory success factors for the position and passed that information on to your organization's Human Resources department. The Human Resources department, in turn, announced the opening internally, placed appropriate advertisements in local newspapers, and notified area headhunters.

Suddenly, a deluge of resumés arrives on your desk. Now what?

It's time to begin the selection process.

First, don't panic. The fact that you've received a number of resumés is good news. Not only do you have a job that's of interest to a number of people, but you also have a large pool of potential candidates to select from. Consider yourself fortunate.

Begin reviewing resumés and selecting applicants for further consideration. Keep in mind that the more time you spend selecting applicants, the higher the quality of your final group of candidates (those who will receive an interview) will be.

CAUTION

> A human resources professional should screen resumés before they reach the desk of the hiring manager. Information contained in the resumé that violates Equal Employment Opportunity Commission (EEOC) or Human Rights standards should be blacked out or otherwise eliminated. (See Lesson 9, "Navigating the Legal Minefield.")

CAUTION

> Since photos included with a resumé provide an unwritten source of inappropriate information (gender, race, age, etc.), they should be immediately returned to the candidate by the Human Resource department.

THE RESUMÉ: WHAT IT IS—AND ISN'T

In Latin the words *curriculum vitae* mean "course of life." That's precisely what a resumé should be: the story of the applicant's life as it pertains to education and work experience.

The resumé is your first opportunity to identify an applicant who may have the experience and training you're looking for. A few words of caution are in order before you begin, however.

First, don't be too impressed with slick resumés that appear to have been professionally designed. The other day, I went to a local office supply store and counted 11 different pieces of resumé-producing software for sale. Each manufacturer boasted of its product's ability to produce print-shop quality resumés in a matter of minutes. Sharp-looking resumés are the norm today, not the exception. Anybody can produce one.

Second, don't be overly impressed with a resumé that's filled with fashionable buzzwords and terms that appear to have been written by someone of superior intellect. The truth is that in the cybersurfing age in which we live, anyone who is willing to spend a few minutes surfing the Web can easily glean all the *technospeak* necessary to write an impressive resumé.

PLAIN ENGLISH

Technospeak   Words and phrases that are particularly in
vogue within special segments of society but that are
not generally understood or recognized by outsiders. For
example, in the field of human resource management,
the term Bi-Polar refers to specific pairs of a candidate's
core strengths; in the field of mental health, that same
term refers to a specific mental health diagnosis.

Third, understand that statements made by an applicant on a resumé
cannot always be taken as absolute truth. Remember that resumés
have a natural bias in favor of applicants. To get their foot in the door,
some applicants think nothing at all of spicing up their resumés by
using highly imaginative ways to promote their perceived strengths,
abilities, and competencies. In fact, some studies suggest that as many
as 30 percent of all resumés contain information that is blatantly false
and misleading.

Keep in mind that, from the standpoint of an applicant, the purpose of a
resumé is to help him or her stand out in competitive hiring situations.
Many job seekers today have been trained to think of their resumés as
personal marketing tools designed to impress prospective employers.

Pertinent facts stated on a resumé, including degrees, licenses, and
experience, ultimately need to be verified before an employment offer
is made. Use the Resumé Review Grid in Appendix C as a guide in
the screening process.

However, for initial screening purposes, in which the goal is simply to
select applicants for further consideration, you should accept information provided in the resumé at face value and evaluate it accordingly.

THE RESUMÉ REVIEW GRID

The right tool always helps you to do a job well. That's certainly true
when it comes to reviewing resumés.

I suggest that you develop a tool to help you with this important task. A simple Resumé Review Grid, with the candidate's name on the left and the selection criteria across the top of the page (as in the accompanying figure), will do the job.

Resume´ Review Grid
Technical Competencies

Candidate	MBA Degree	Required Experience	Desktop Publishing	Training Experience	Hiring Experience	Budgeting Experience	Total
John Doe	x	x		3	3	5	**11xx**
Al Green		x	5	5	4	5	**19x**
Mary Smith	x	x	4	5	3	4	**16xx**
Paul Jones	x	x		4	2	3	**9xx**
Betty Brown		x	4	5	4	2	**15x**
Jim Peterson		x	2	3	3		**8x**

Functional Skills

Candidate	Analysis	Supervision	Management	Innovation	Total
John Doe	5	4	3	5	**17**
Al Green	3	5	4	4	**16**
Mary Smith	5	4	5	5	**19**
Paul Jones	2	1	3	4	**10**
Betty Brown	3	4	5	5	**17**
Jim Peterson	2	1	2	4	**9**

Recap

Candidate	Total
John Doe	**28xx**
Al Green	**35x**
Mary Smith	**35xx**
Paul Jones	**19xx**
Betty Brown	**32x**
Jim Peterson	**17x**

A sample of the Resumé Review Grid.

Under each criterion, allow room for a rating number of 0 to 5 (5 being the optimal score). Selection criteria that involve special education, licensing, or degrees would simply be checked in the appropriate area of the grid.

On the right side of the grid, designate a column for the total score achieved by the applicant. Check marks should be carried over and included with totals to indicate that, in addition to the numeric score, other specific selection criteria have been met. Leave the bottom of the sheet open for evaluator comments and notes.

Give each evaluator a copy of the resumé, together with the Resumé Review Grid. After evaluations have been completed, prepare a Master Resumé Review Grid for each applicant, showing the average score achieved for each selection criterion as well as an overall average score.

Offer personal interviews to those applicants who score highest. Note questions and comments made by the evaluators, and explore them further with the applicant in person.

NARROWING THE FIELD

At this juncture in the hiring process, narrow the field of applicants to those whose resumés demonstrate the likelihood that they possess the appropriate qualifications. Your time and the time of those who help you interview candidates is valuable. You don't want to waste it with applicants who obviously are not qualified to do the job.

But be careful about the reasons that you use to disqualify applicants from further consideration. Make sure that your reasons for rejection are firmly rooted in the requirements of the job, not in anything extraneous. Also, be sure to thoroughly document your reasons for disqualification. A copy of the Resumé Review Grid, together with any notes concerning the disqualified applicant's resumé, should be attached to the resumé and kept on file.

To ensure objectivity, ask those who will later serve on your interview team to help review resumés and select applicants. Not only will you be assured of a better, more objective result, but you also will make a legal challenge by a disgruntled applicant more difficult to conduct. Shared decision making, especially in hiring matters, is always best.

CAUTION

If the job requires a degree or other special education, make sure that such requirements are essential to the successful performance of the job. Requirements of this nature can be considered discriminatory because they may have a disproportionate impact to certain segments of the population. For example, the EEOC has held that employment decisions based upon the credit history of a candidate will have a disparate impact on minority candidates because a disproportionate number of minorities live below the poverty level.

ZEROING IN

You should consider three parts of the resumé in the preinterview selection phase:

- Education and training
- Experience
- Personal information

EDUCATION AND TRAINING

This portion of the resumé catalogs the applicant's formal education. Some applicants will also list seminars and workshops attended, especially when such programs have direct application to the job being sought. Applicants should furnish information concerning dates of graduation or completion, as well as dates that degrees were conferred.

Look for education and training that meets the requirements of the position. Be sure to note any questions or concerns that you may have so that you can ask the applicant for clarification or further information during the interview.

TIP

Consider whether the position really requires a degree. Filling a position with someone who is overqualified for the job ensures rapid turnover.

EXPERIENCE

Experience is the most significant portion of the resumé in the preinterview selection phase. Here you'll find the particulars about an applicant's work experience and qualifications.

In evaluating the experience of an applicant, be sure to do the following:

- Look for job descriptions that have particular relevance to the position that you hope to fill.

- Consider the level of the applicant's prior experience. Is it above or below that required for the job for which the candidate is applying?

- Is the applicant's experience written in a clear, concise manner, or are the terms used particularly vague and confusing?

- Based on the applicant's experience, does it appear that he or she possesses the mandatory success factors discussed in Lesson 1, "Analyzing the Position"?

PERSONAL INFORMATION

Personal information contained in a resumé can be of exceptional value in your preinterview screening process. Information such as personal interests, extracurricular activities, and civic involvements provide a glimpse into a candidate's values and ambitions. Leisure pursuits and hobbies that relate to the responsibilities of the position suggest a candidate who is deeply interested and committed to the mission of the job.

GREEN FLAGS, RED FLAGS

A thorough review of most resumés is likely to produce some *green flags* as well as some *red flags*.

PLAIN ENGLISH

> **Green flags**   Items on the resumé that clearly demonstrate positive achievement, especially in areas involving mandatory success factors. **Red flags**   Items that indicate potential problems and mean either that further exploration with the applicant is necessary, or that the resumé can be rejected from further consideration outright.

GREEN FLAGS

Green flags are dazzling indicators that justify further consideration of the candidate. You will want to note any green flags present in an applicant's resumé and consider that information as you select candidates for interview.

Here's a list of some of the more important green flags that strongly suggest real achievement:

- **Career stability**   The candidate's resumé provides evidence of solid commitment to a chosen career path. Job changes have involved progressively more responsibility.

- **Contribution to organization**   The resumé not only discusses job responsibilities, but it also talks about contributions that the candidate made to organizations as a result of meeting or exceeding expectations.

- **Determination** The resumé reflects the applicant's strong desire and ambition to move forward. Duties and responsibilities listed for previous work demonstrate that the applicant accepted challenges beyond those normally associated with the nature of the job.

- **Dreams and aspirations** The resumé demonstrates that the candidate wants to accomplish something great and has the vision to realize his or her dreams. A resumé that states a career objective well above and beyond the position applied for can reveal a candidate whose dreams and aspirations are in focus.

Red Flags

You will also encounter some red flags as you review the resumés of potential candidates. That's to be expected.

Red flags signal possible problems. Note each red flag you find on the candidate's resumé review grid. Red flags may indicate a need for more information or clarification from the applicant. Or, they may signal a genuine cause for concern.

Whatever you do, don't ignore red flags. Here are some common ones:

- Unexplained gaps in employment history. These may simply be errors in the chronology of the resumé, or they may signal the possibility of more serious concerns.

- Frequent job changes that are obviously not promotions or better opportunities may signal a variety of work-related problems. Does the applicant have difficulty taking direction? Or, is there a problem getting along with co-workers?

- Overuse of terms such as "knowledge of," "experience with," "understanding of," "exposure to," and "familiarity with." These are terms frequently used by those who lack the kind of hands-on experience required.

- Experience or education listed in something other than chronological order. Resumés using functional formats in which prior experience is emphasized often ignore dates completely and are frequently used to hide significant gaps.

- Resumés that criticize former employers or supervisors may signal serious attitude problems. A resumé should be a vehicle used to sell the skills and experience of an applicant, not to trash former employers.

THE RESUMÉ AND THE INTERVIEW

The resumé is an important document. It provides pertinent information about qualifications of applicants for positions in your organization.

It's important to remember, however, that the interview itself should be devoted to behavioral questions that seek to measure a candidate's skills and abilities as they relate to the identified mandatory success factors. The interview is not the time to rehash the resumé point by point.

THE 30-SECOND RECAP

- Pizzazz is no substitute for substance—resumés should present an applicant's qualifications in a straightforward chronological manner.

- Develop a simple Resumé Review Grid that will help evaluators assess resumés fairly.

- The same team members who will participate in the interview process should also review resumés.

- Be sure to note all green flags and red flags that are uncovered in the initial review.

- Don't rehash resumés during interviews.

Lesson 3
References

In this lesson, you learn how to obtain good reference information that will help you conduct a more meaningful interview. You also learn what questions you can legally ask and what areas to avoid.

Why Check References?

Of all the tasks associated with hiring new employees, checking references has historically ranked among the least favored. All too often, managers don't bother to contact former employers because they think that reference checks are an exercise in futility. Some studies by the American Management Association estimate that the references of as many as 70 percent of all new hires were never checked. Big mistake.

Here are the two best reasons I know for conscientiously checking the references of prospective employees:

- Reference checks help prevent lawsuits for negligent hiring.

- Reference checks help prevent costly hiring mistakes.

Negligent Hiring

Workplace crime involving assault, terrorism, fraud, arson, theft, and even murder is on the rise. In fact, statistical evidence from the United States Department of Labor identifies violence in the workplace as one of the fastest-growing causes of death on the job. Moreover, studies seem to demonstrate a strong correlation between past criminal activity and job-related crime.

Most states have already adopted the legal doctrine of *"negligent hiring"* and "negligent retention." These legal theories maintain that an employer is liable for the harmful acts of an employee if the employer knew—or should have known—of similar incidents in the employee's background. An employer's negligence is based on the fact that, had the employer done an adequate job of evaluating and investigating the applicant, the harm would not have occurred.

PLAIN ENGLISH

> **Negligent hiring**   The failure to exercise a reasonable amount of care in recruiting and selecting a candidate for a job, which ultimately results in injury or damage to another.

In the past, employers were considered liable for the acts of an employee while performing the duties of the job. Today, under the tort of negligent hiring, employers are liable for the harmful acts of an employee even when those acts are beyond the scope of the job.

The legal adage remains true: The best defense is a good offense. Thoroughly checking an applicant's employment history and personal references is the best way to keep your workplace safe and avoid becoming embroiled in costly negligent hiring claims.

DECREASING HIRING MISTAKES

CAUTION

> Regardless of how impressive a candidate may seem, always verify academic credentials and check the references provided. No exceptions.

Hiring mistakes are expensive. They take a major toll on an organization's finances and employee morale.

A few years ago, a Minnesota firm hired a chief financial officer whose resumé stated that he had graduated with honors from a prestigious Ivy League university with an advanced degree in accounting. The candidate had interviewed well and had impressed management with his prestigious background.

Management was so convinced he was the right man for the job that they immediately offered him an excellent salary and benefit package, and included some truly exceptional perks such as a liberal stock option arrangement. But in their rush to fill the position, no one bothered to verify the individual's educational credentials.

Almost two years later, a federally mandated audit revealed that the company's financial records were in a state of absolute disarray. That's when the board of directors decided to take another look at the resumé of their CFO. When they contacted the Ivy League university listed on it, they learned that the closest this individual ever got to the prestigious campus was, in all likelihood, driving down the freeway that passed nearby.

The result: embarrassed managers, an irate board of directors, a demoralized staff, the loss of a federal contract worth more than a million dollars, and an expense of $185,000 for an outside accounting firm to repair the company's financial records. And all of it could have been prevented with a five-minute phone call to the Ivy League university to verify a degree.

Will performing thorough reference checks keep you from making hiring mistakes? No. But your percentage of bad hires will decline significantly. In fact, some informal research conducted by my organization suggests that as many as 85 percent of hiring mistakes can be avoided by thorough reference checks.

Reference checks present a genuine opportunity to learn more about an applicant. Former employers are in the best position to provide useful information about a candidate's skills, abilities, prior work performance, and character.

TIP

Consider asking candidates to submit as many as ten "personal" references that may include previous employers. That way, when you contact a former employer, you can truthfully explain that the applicant provided his or her name as a "personal" reference (instead of as a former employer or business reference). This approach usually yields better information, and more of it.

THE CONSPIRACY OF SILENCE

Getting previous employers to level with you about an ex-employee may prove difficult. Conspiracies of silence are very real. In many organizations, *disclosure agreements* make it next to impossible for previous employers to speak candidly about former workers.

PLAIN ENGLISH

Disclosure agreement   A legally binding agreement between an employer and an employee who is leaving the organization. The agreement purposely limits the information that can later be disclosed to prospective employers.

Whether or not employees leave under less than favorable circumstances, disclosure agreements are often used to limit the information that former employers can disclose. Some employers adhere to the "name, rank, and serial number" approach, providing only minimal information. It's not uncommon for such firms to restrict disclosable information to dates of employment, job title of the last position held, final salary, and a touch of murky narrative that has been carefully worded and mutually agreed upon concerning the character of the employee and the general quality of work that he or she performed.

The use of disclosure agreements is motivated by the fear of costly, and often well-publicized, defamation or invasion of privacy litigation.

Ex-employees sometimes sue former employers, claiming substantial damages as a result of negative reference reports. Juries in many of these cases have been sympathetic to employees, handing down megadollar judgments against corporate defendants.

Here are some suggestions that will help you in your quest for meaningful reference information. Think about implementing them in your organization:

- Always have applicants complete an application that grants permission to contact references. A resumé is not an application. Be sure that your application contains an authorization permitting you to contact any and all former employers and others who have knowledge of the applicant's work history, experience and education, and that allows them to provide information about the applicant.

- Include a "hold harmless" agreement with your employment application that will prevent former employers from being sued by an applicant as a result of releasing reference information. Then send a copy of the signed agreement to each reference before contacting them. Hold harmless agreements can go a long way in lowering the guard of former employers.

- Check references *before* interviewing those you've selected for further consideration. Having done so will not only provide a better understanding of each applicant, but it may also direct you to areas that require further exploration.

- Check references yourself—don't assign the task to others. Managers will have more success talking with other managers. Also, by contacting references directly, the manager can *listen intuitively* to what is (and is not) being said.

- Be sure to ask each reference for the names of others in the organization who may be familiar with the qualifications of the applicant. It's astonishing how much information you can obtain from those whose names weren't provided by an applicant.

- Share the information received from reference checks with other members of the interview panel.

- Always contact colleges and universities to verify degrees. The most common form of deception involves applicants who overstate educational accomplishments. Colleges and universities are eager to provide information about the academic achievements of former students. It's fast and easy information to obtain.

- Document all information that you receive. Your documentation will be vital if you ever have to defend your actions.

- Don't contact only one or two references. Make it a practice to contact all of them, without fail. And be sure to ask each reference to provide you with the names of others who have knowledge of the applicant's skills and work experience.

PLAIN ENGLISH

Intuitive listening   Being sensitive both to what is said and to what is *not* said. It is the message conveyed by a hesitation, a reluctance to discuss a matter, or an obvious desire to change the subject.

THE RIGHT QUESTIONS

The quality of information that you receive from references depends upon how well you ask questions. Here are a few things to remember:

- Don't ask leading questions that provide the reference with the information given by the applicant. Instead of asking, "Mr. Peterson said that you worked in his unit for 5 years. Is that correct?" ask instead, "How long did you work for Mr. Peterson?" Let the reference provide the information.

- Don't ask closed-ended questions (questions that can be answered with a simple "yes" or "no"). You want to hear what the references have to say. Give them a chance to speak freely without limiting their replies.

- Be sure to ask questions that verify basic facts such as dates of employment, salary, title of last position, duties, and so on.

- Limit your questions to those that directly relate to an applicant's qualifications for the job (that is, the mandatory success factors—see Lesson 1, "Analyzing the Position").

QUESTIONS YOU CAN'T ASK

Some questions you can't ask when talking to references. Questions regarding any of the following categories are illegal:

- Age

- Race

- Religion

- Marital status

- Children or childcare arrangements

- Pregnancy or family plans

- Sexual orientation

- Parents of the applicant

- Medical status, disabilities, or impairments

- Psychological or physical well-being

- Residence

- Membership in social organizations

- Union membership

- Previous use of drugs and alcohol

- Arrest record

- Visible characteristics

In addition to these, a prospective employer is prohibited by law from asking a reference (including former employers) anything that the employer is prohibited from asking the applicant directly (see Lesson 9, "Navigating the Legal Minefield").

METHODS OF INTERVIEWING REFERENCES

There are three primary methods of interviewing references—by mail, by telephone, and through the use of a private search firm

REFERENCES BY MAIL

Requesting references by mail (or e-mail) is decidedly the poorest method. It always results in the fewest responses. Those replies you do receive are likely to be written in an extremely guarded fashion.

Why? Written information about an ex-employee can easily be construed as demeaning and can become the basis for litigation against the former employer. Even when the intent was to provide a positive reference, certain words or phrases can imply something else. Most former employers simply avoid responding in this manner.

Use mail to send references a personal note informing them that John or Jane Doe has applied for a position with your firm and has given you their name as a personal reference. Inform the reference that you will be phoning in the next few days to talk about the qualifications of the applicant. Be sure to include a copy of the applicant's consent form and hold harmless agreement. This helps set the stage for the reference interview and knocks down barriers in advance.

REFERENCES BY TELEPHONE

The telephone is by far the most common way of obtaining references. It's fast, inexpensive, and effective.

Begin your phone conversation with a reference by referring to the letter that you sent earlier, together with the consent and waiver signed by the applicant: "John Doe gave me your name as a personal reference and asked me to phone you. Is now a good time to talk, or would you prefer that I phone later today?"

Get the details out of the way first. Start by asking questions that verify factual data. Ask for dates of employment, title of the applicant's last position with the firm, salary information, duties and responsibilities of the job, and so on.

After the preliminary information has been gathered, tell the reference a little about the job for which the applicant is being considered and the requirements of that job. Use the mandatory success factors that you developed in Lesson 1 to formulate specific *probes*. Consider these examples:

- Can you tell me about a time when Pete had to use his problem-solving skills? (problem solving)

- What did Mary do to contribute to an environment of teamwork in your organization? (team building)

- Can you tell me about a time when Helen positively influenced the action of others? (leadership)

- What was the most creative thing Bill did while he worked for your company? (creativity)

PLAIN ENGLISH

Probe   A question or request that seeks specific information, clarification, or confirmation from a candidate being interviewed. Probes may be open or closed depending on the purpose.

USING SEARCH FIRMS

Many firms today specialize in checking the backgrounds of applicants for employment. Many of them have an Internet presence, and their services can be obtained electronically.

Most search firms perform in-depth interviews with previous employers, check educational credentials, and confirm dates of attendance and degrees earned at any institution of higher education. Some will even check the credit of applicants, obtain motor vehicle reports, and perform criminal background checks (if appropriate).

Typically, these services are fast and relatively inexpensive, and provide professional reports of their findings. However, in my opinion, they are a poor substitute for personal contact by a prospective employer. Be careful about delegating this important task to an unknown investigator.

And, incidentally, if you think that by using a professional search firm you somehow diminish your potential legal liability in a negligent hiring lawsuit, think again. A firm that you hire to help gather information about an applicant becomes your legal agent. You remain responsible for the completeness and accuracy of the information used to make employment decisions.

TALKING WITH PRESENT EMPLOYERS

It's common practice for applicants to ask you not to contact current employers. Until they find what they're looking for, applicants often don't want it known that they're searching for another job. That's understandable.

Although it's important to honor such a wish, it's also important to protect your interests. I suggest that in these instances, you make it clear to an applicant that any offer of employment would be contingent upon a satisfactory reference from the current employer. If the current employer provides a less-than-satisfactory reference, the offer would be subject to immediate withdrawal. Be sure to include language to this effect in any job offer and letter of confirmation.

Always follow up with a call to the present employer after a conditional offer of employment is made and accepted. Don't neglect talking to the person who has the most current information about your candidate and is in the best position to discuss his or her skills and abilities.

CREDIT CHECKS

If personal financial conduct is relevant to the job for which an applicant is being considered, consumer credit reports can be an important source of information. However, on September 30, 1997, the Fair

Credit Reporting Act was amended to include strict notice requirements whenever credit reports for employment purposes are sought. Under present law, an employer must do the following:

- Notify an applicant in writing before a consumer credit report is procured, stating that such a report may be obtained for employment purposes.

- Obtain the applicant's written authorization to procure such a report.

- Provide the applicant with a copy of the report, together with a description of the applicant's rights under the Fair Credit Reporting Act *before* taking adverse action based in whole or in part on the report.

- Refrain from taking adverse action based in whole or in part on the report until the applicant has had sufficient time to respond to any discrepancies in the report.

An investigative consumer credit report that involves questioning friends and neighbors of the applicant may also be used to obtain important background information. A written notice must be sent to the applicant within three days of requesting the report. In addition, the applicant must be informed of his or her right to demand disclosure of the nature and scope of the investigative report and to receive a written summary of his or her rights under the law.

CAUTION

The use of consumer credit information in making employment decisions is legal. However, exercise extreme caution in using this information. Credit information can have a disparate impact on minority or women applicants and can provide a basis for litigation against employers. The likelihood of becoming embroiled in litigation is enhanced by the notice requirements of the law. Consult your corporate attorney before obtaining credit information and using it to qualify or disqualify an applicant.

PLAIN ENGLISH

Disparate impact   A term used by the United States Supreme Court in a 1977 case involving the International Brotherhood of Teamsters. According to the court, disparate impact results from employment practices that appear to be neutral in their treatment of different groups, but that actually impact one group more harshly than another and cannot be justified by business necessity.

CRIMINAL BACKGROUND CHECKS

Obtaining information about an applicant's prior arrests can be problematic. Some states prohibit employers from accessing such information.

But the real concern is with the federal law. Members of minority groups have been effective in asserting that their groups are over-represented in the population with arrest records. If this fact can be demonstrated by state or local statistical evidence, chances are good that inquiries into the arrest records of an applicant of the minority group involved will violate federal law.

Most states allow prospective employers to inquire about felony convictions. However, not all states allow employers to deny employment on the basis of a felony conviction.

Exercise care if you intend to use information about an applicant's record of arrest and conviction. Remember that you are likely restricted by state or federal law in the way you can use the information. Consult your organization's legal counsel to determine the advisability of performing criminal background checks and to learn what restrictions apply to you.

Driving Records

If a prospective employee's duties include driving, checking motor vehicle records may be in order. But access to this type of information is often limited and difficult to obtain. And obtaining motor vehicle records in other states presents an even greater challenge since each state has its own regulations governing the release of such information.

The 30-Second Recap

- Thorough reference checks can prevent negligent hiring lawsuits and reduce hiring mistakes by as much as 85 percent.

- Ask for ten "personal" references that may include former employers.

- Ask each preselected applicant to complete a formal job application that contains written permission for you to contact references and others having knowledge of previous work, and that allows others to release information to you.

- Consider developing (with the help of your legal department) a hold harmless agreement that would prevent former employers from being sued by an applicant as a result of releasing reference information.

- Make it a practice to phone each reference provided by the applicant before an interview.

- Network references by asking each reference for the names of others who have firsthand knowledge of the applicant's work.

- Make your job offer contingent on a positive reference from a present employer.

- Use credit checks, criminal background inquiries, and checks of driving records only after receiving legal guidance from your corporate attorney.

LESSON 4
Testing

In this lesson, you learn to obtain factual data about how an applicant is likely to perform on the job by means of various tests.

THE MARVEL OF PRE-EMPLOYMENT TESTING

We live in a marvelous age. Almost every week we learn of wonderful new scientific discoveries to help us live longer or enhance the quality of our lives.

Employment testing has also benefited from years of scientific research. Today, pre-employment testing offers a valid, objective way to predict the suitability of a candidate for a particular job. And here's a bonus: Information obtained through testing will help you zero in on important areas to explore further during the interview.

CAUTION

If you opt for pre-employment testing, be sure to test each qualified applicant before the interview. Testing that is done following an interview and limited to only a few finalists may well be considered discriminatory.

You should know about five basic types of pre-employment tests:

- Aptitude and intelligence tests
- Behavior tests
- Technical skills testing
- Clinical evaluations
- Pop psychology tests

APTITUDE AND INTELLIGENCE TESTS

The purpose of aptitude testing is to predict an applicant's general level of future performance. Most of us have had experience taking some kind of aptitude test. For example, chances are, in high school you took the Scholastic Aptitude Test (SAT) to determine the likelihood of your success in college; before entering graduate school, you probably were required to take a Graduate Record Examination (GRE); if you went to law school, the Law School Admission Test (LSAT) was a requirement. Each of these aptitude tests predicted your performance in the future.

Tests of intelligence (or IQ tests) assess an individual's mental ability, as well as his or her intellectual capacity to reason and apply skills and knowledge. Two of the most widely used tests for this purpose are these:

- The Stanford-Binet test
- The Wechsler Adult Intelligence Scale

Administration of either of these tests requires specific training and, in many states, a license. Other tests of this nature are on the market today and can also do admirable jobs of measuring a candidate's intelligence.

Why are tests of intelligence important? In an article published in *Fortune* magazine, James Q. Wilson, professor of management at the University of California, Los Angeles, reviewed the book *A Question of Intelligence: The IQ Debate in America*, by Daniel Seligman (New York: Carol Publishing [Birch Lane Press], 1992). Professor Wilson wrote:

> People who mistakenly think that "intelligence is only what intelligence tests test" will be surprised to learn how powerfully IQ predicts not only school achievement but also job performance—even in jobs that don't require people to engage mostly in "mental" activities. Soldiers firing tank guns are more likely to hit their targets if they have higher IQs. Bright police officers make better cops than not-so-bright ones. Professor John E. Hunter of Michigan State concluded after surveying the abundant evidence on this matter that there are no jobs for which intelligence tests do not predict performance. Of

course, other factors, such as personality and work habits, also make a difference, but IQ is emphatically not just a matter of being "good with words."

Intelligence tests are exceptional predictors of future performance. Consider taking advantage of them.

But be careful in your selection of tests. Be sure that the test you use to measure aptitude and intelligence has been professionally developed and that there is evidence that test results are *valid and reliable*.

PLAIN ENGLISH

Valid and reliable   These two words have special meanings in the world of testing. Validity refers to the extent that a given test actually measures what it is designed to measure. Reliability refers to the consistency of scores and measurement that is free of error.

BEHAVIOR TESTS

Behavior tests operate in the *soft area of measurement*. They predict an applicant's behavior on the job by exploring motivation, personality patterns or problems, and interpersonal skills. This information can be helpful in gaining a better understanding of the applicant and in preparing to interview him or her.

PLAIN ENGLISH

Soft measurements   Tests and inventories based mostly on self-reporting, beliefs and feelings, or past behavior. There are no right or wrong answers.

It is essential, however, to determine exactly what personality traits are applicable to the job. The mandatory success factors that you've discovered through your assessment of the job (see Lesson 1, "Analyzing the Position") will suggest personality traits and interpersonal abilities that should be measured.

Information about a candidate derived from behavior testing will help keep your interview focused on important issues. Concerns identified by testing signal the need to probe certain areas more thoroughly in the interview.

CAUTION

Although some employers insist on selecting and administering pre-employment tests themselves, psychological testing is best left to professionals. Industrial psychologists are trained to select testing that measures specific criteria (mandatory success factors), and are skilled in administering tests and interpreting results.

TIP

The cost of testing, compared to the value of the information received, is money well spent. The cost for testing alone is generally much less than the cost of a comprehensive psychological assessment.

TECHNICAL SKILLS TESTS

Technical skills tests are tests that are best performed in the natural work environment. These tests are designed to measure an applicant's ability to perform a specific task.

For example, a keyboarding test (formerly known as a typing test) measures an applicant's ability to produce a certain number of correct words per minute. Similar tests may seek to measure proficiency with various computer programs, or the ability to operate certain machinery or equipment.

CLINICAL EVALUATIONS

A comprehensive clinical evaluation by a licensed industrial psychologist involves a combination of tests and interviews with the applicant.

These evaluations are usually reserved for applicants contending for key management positions with an organization.

Comprehensive evaluations are thorough and require a significant amount of professional time to complete. The cost is usually between $500 and $1,200, depending on location.

The employer furnishes the psychologist with a complete description of the job, along with its mandatory success factors. The psychologist selects tests and inventories that probe critical areas and performs in-depth interviews with applicants designed to confirm and supplement test results. Upon completion of the evaluation, the employer is usually provided with a multipage narrative report discussing the fitness of the applicant for the job.

POP PSYCHOLOGY TESTS

It never ceases to amaze me how many pop psychological tests appear on the market each year. Given the litigious nature of the society in which we live, it's difficult to imagine that anyone would risk using any instrument that has a questionable or nonexistent foundation in research.

Be careful. Pre-employment testing is, first and foremost, the practice of psychology. Let me say it again: Unless you have the requisite training and license, it's best to leave the practice of psychology to psychologists.

ARE PRE-EMPLOYMENT TESTS LEGAL?

The answer is not as uncomplicated as it may seem. Under present federal law, and in view of relevant Supreme Court decisions, it's fair to say that pre-employment tests are legal, provided that the following is true:

- The tests measure factors involved in the specific job for which the applicant is being considered. This point is important. A test that has only limited relationship or application to the job may result in a lawsuit for discrimination.

- The tests have been professionally developed, and ample research exists demonstrating the tests to be valid and reliable in the testing of job candidates.

- Testing is not conducted in a discriminatory fashion. All applicants for the job who pass initial screenings for qualification should be given an opportunity to demonstrate their competence and ability by participating in pre-employment testing.

CAUTION

Employers should also be aware that even when extreme caution has been taken to ensure that tests meet legal requirements, they could still be challenged under a disparate impact theory. An applicant can allege that test questions had a disparate impact on a protected group of which they are part (women, minorities, disabled individuals, people over 40 years of age, and so on).

The type of tests least likely to produce a legal challenge are tests that measure technical skills. These are easily validated and usually involve the measurement of skills directly related to the job. Validation of other, more subjective, tests is much more difficult and demands the services of a highly trained professional psychologist.

OTHER KINDS OF PRE-EMPLOYMENT TESTS

Listed here are a few other kinds of pre-employment tests and evaluations that employers often ask about. It's important to understand the potential legal consequences of using each of them in the selection process.

- Medical examinations
- Polygraph examinations
- Drug and alcohol tests
- Genetic tests

Medical Examinations

It is unlawful to require an applicant to take a medical examination in the *preoffer stage* of the employment selection process. Prospective employers may not even so much as make inquiries into the medical history of an applicant at this juncture. That's because the EEOC broadly defines "medical examination" to mean any procedure or test that seeks information about an individual's physical or mental impairments or health.

PLAIN ENGLISH

> **Preoffer stage**   That period in the selection process before the employer extends a conditional offer of employment to an applicant.

Questions concerning disability or about the nature and severity of a disability are also unlawful. Employers may ask questions about the applicant's ability to perform certain job-related functions, as long as the questions are not phrased in terms of a disability.

Also, employers may request applicants to perform physical agility tests that demonstrate their ability to do the job for which they are applying. However, any attempt to determine a physiological condition based on such a test would be considered a medical examination under EEOC guidelines and, therefore, would be prohibited.

In the *postoffer stage* of the selection process, an applicant can be asked to submit to a thorough medical examination. At this time, employers may also make disability-related inquiries.

PLAIN ENGLISH

> **Postoffer stage**   That stage of the selection process when a conditional offer of employment has been extended to an applicant. Conditional offers are made when present employers have yet to be contacted, or when the offer is subject to the applicant passing a medical examination.

CAUTION

To avoid claims of discrimination, employers must treat all applicants the same. If one prospective employee is required to pass a medical examination before a firm offer of employment is extended, every applicant for a job in that same category must also be required to pass the same medical examination.

One more important consideration: If a prospective employee is eliminated as a result of medical or disability information, the criteria used to exclude the prospective worker must be job-related and based on business necessity. Furthermore, an employer must be able to demonstrate that the essential functions of the job could not be performed by the employee even with a reasonable accommodation on the part of the employer.

POLYGRAPH EXAMINATIONS

The use of polygraph examinations in the selection process has been the subject of litigation. Courts have consistently held that the use of polygraph examinations in this manner is illegal unless the employer is one that is specifically exempted by the Employee Polygraph Protection Act. The Act exempts employers who provide private security services and employers who manufacture, distribute, or dispense controlled substances.

Not long ago, the city of Long Beach, California, began a practice of requiring pre-employment polygraph examinations for all job applicants. City officials ordered the change in employment policy after discovering some money missing from city property.

The Long Beach City Employees Association sued the city but lost in Superior Court. However, the Supreme Court of California reversed the lower court's decision on appeal. The Supreme Court said that the city's policy on polygraph evaluations violated the prospective employee's right to privacy. The court further ruled that the city failed to prove a compelling interest to public safety that would necessitate polygraph testing, and questioned the reliability of the polygraph itself.

Polygraph examinations of existing staff are also prohibited. The Employee Polygraph Protection Act specifically prohibits demanding that present employees submit to polygraph examination. There are some exceptions, but they are few.

My advice if you're considering including a polygraph examination as a testing device: Forget it. Employers who violate the federal law are subject to a fine of $10,000 for each occurrence and, in addition, can be sued by the individuals involved.

DRUG TESTS

Drug tests are permissible in the preoffer stage as long as the employer provides prior written notice to applicants. Employers must also be prepared to demonstrate that a drug test is required of all applicants who reach the preoffer stage.

The EEOC has made it clear that anyone who is currently using illegal drugs is not protected by the Americans with Disabilities Act and may be denied employment (or fired, if already employed) on the basis of such use. Also, a test for illegal use of drugs is not considered a medical examination, and employers are not required to demonstrate that the drug test is job-related and consistent with business necessity.

If the testing laboratory notifies the employer that a drug test was positive for a controlled substance, the employer should discuss the result with the applicant to determine if there is some reasonable explanation (the applicant is taking prescribed drugs which are controlled substances under the care of a physician, for example).

If an applicant cannot provide a reasonable explanation for the positive drug screen, an employer is justified in withdrawing the conditional offer of employment.

CAUTION

> Employers should consult their legal advisers about any
> changes that may occur in federal regulations pertaining
> to drug testing. State law may also dictate conditions
> under which drug tests may be required of prospective
> employees.

GENETIC TESTING

As I write this book, one of the greatest discoveries of our age was
announced. Scientists involved in the Human Genome Project have
announced that they have successfully "cracked" the human genetic
code. This means that the locations and functions of human genes
that code for inherited genetic traits have been discovered and
mapped.

Although I'm no scientist, it seems clear that understanding the human
genetic code has vast implications in the field of modern medicine. An
individual's risk of falling victim to a genetically influenced disease
may now be able to be identified early and treated proactively by
altering the gene in question.

One of the unresolved issues that surrounds this discovery has to do
with the use of genetic information in the workplace. Genetic information reveals predisposition to certain traits or disorders—should
employers be allowed access to test results in considering applicants
for employment? Should they be permitted to deny employment on
the basis of genetic testing? Should employers be allowed to use
genetic information to determine jobs best suited for an individual?

The legal and ethical implications of this research are overwhelming,
challenging public policymakers to think beyond traditional legal and
ethical paradigms.

Under current regulations, genetic testing would likely fall under the
ADA's broad definition of "medical examination." If this is true,
employers may require applicants in the postoffer stage to undergo

genetic testing, as long as employers meet three basic conditions set by the ADA:

1. The employer must require that all new employees submit to genetic testing regardless of disability.

2. The employer must maintain a separate confidential file containing the results of genetic tests.

3. The employer can reject an applicant only if genetic test results clearly demonstrate that such a decision would be "job-related and consistent with business necessity."

All this seems like a page out of Aldous Huxley's *Utopia*, in which science controls the destiny of humankind and an individual's genetic blueprint determines his or her fate. Without doubt, there is a dark side to genetic testing.

THE 30-SECOND RECAP

- Pre-employment tests should be done before the interview to prevent claims of discrimination and to help focus the interview on important areas that may require further exploration.

- Aptitude tests, behavior tests, and intelligence tests are best selected and administered by a trained, licensed psychologist who specializes in employment testing.

- Pre-employment testing is legal as long as the tests involved are job-specific, are professionally developed, have proven validity, and are not conducted in a discriminatory fashion.

- Understanding what can be required of an applicant in the preoffer and postoffer stages of the selection process is important.

- Specific regulations apply to other forms of pre-employment tests, including medical examinations, polygraph tests, drug tests, and genetic tests.

LESSON 5
Interview Models

In this lesson, you learn about the major types of interviews commonly used in the hiring process, and the advantages and disadvantages of each.

MUTUAL EXPLORATION

The primary purpose of a job interview is mutual exploration. The employer wants to discover more about an applicant's qualifications for a job; the applicant wants to discover more about the employer as well as the opportunity that the employer has to offer. The exploration is a learning process for both parties, each of whom develops understandings and expectations.

The employer can use several interview formats. Each, in its own way, fosters mutual exploration. Each format is designed to elicit specific information about a candidate's qualifications for the job while affording the candidate an opportunity to ask pertinent questions of the employer. However, the formats differ significantly in the way they accomplish these goals. As a result, the type and quality of information obtained can vary from format to format. Selecting the right format for an interview is crucial to hiring the right person for the job.

TYPES OF INTERVIEWS

The interview formats commonly used in the selection process include these:

- Telephone screening interview
- Traditional interview

- Stress interview

- Team interview

- Situational interview

- Structured behavioral interview

TELEPHONE INTERVIEW

"Hi, I'm Joan Peterson with XYZ Corporation, and I'd like to ask you a few questions about the resumé that you submitted for the position of sales associate with our firm. Do you have a few moments to talk?"

 TIP

> Use telephone interviews as part of your "narrowing the field" activities, discussed in Lesson 2, "The Resumé."

Telephone interviews are primarily used in the preselection phase of the selection process. Their purpose is to narrow the number of applicants who will receive a formal interview by eliminating those who don't have the requisite education, experience, and skills to successfully do the job. Telephone interviews are used to obtain answers to any questions that may be posed by the applicant's resumé, and to obtain additional information about the skills and experience of an applicant.

One advantage of the telephone interview is that it can be accomplished quickly and economically. Without telephone interviews, organizations would be overwhelmed by the task of interviewing candidates face to face who could have been disqualified much earlier in the process.

In a typical telephone interview, the interviewer spends a few minutes explaining the position and how it fits into the organization. The interviewer then asks some predetermined questions about background and education, and attempts to clarify any inconsistencies in the resumé.

Typically, the interviewer inquires whether the applicant has any questions about the position, and concludes the interview by explaining what the applicant can expect to occur next in the selection process. Telephone interviews are usually highly focused and last about 10 to 15 minutes.

CAUTION

> Remember that while you are evaluating applicants by phone, good candidates will also be evaluating you. Be sure to represent your organization well by remaining professional and courteous.

Advantages: Telephone interviews are fast, easy to accomplish, and cost-efficient. They are an effective way to narrow the field of applicants to those who will be offered a personal interview.

Disadvantages: Telephone interviews eliminate the possibility of evaluating an applicant's nonverbal behavior. In addition, it's easy for an interviewer to judge a candidate on the basis of "telephone presence" instead of mandatory success factors. People who would otherwise make excellent candidates may not have good telephone communication skills.

TRADITIONAL INTERVIEW

"Tell us a little about yourself."

The traditional interview is the most common form of interview in small- to medium-sized organizations, and it's not all that uncommon in large organizations and government offices.

Here are some characteristics of the traditional interview:

- Questions are often vague, unfocused, and theoretical.
- Candidates are allowed to theorize and generalize about their background and experience.

- Very few questions have follow-up probes to obtain more specific information.

- Candidates who have become skilled at interviewing often gain control of the interview and tend to redirect attention to areas of their choice.

- Interviewers may take some notes during the interview, but note taking is not tremendously important.

- Interviews can easily drift into rapport-building sessions.

In the traditional format, questions are often predictable, allowing applicants an opportunity to rehearse their responses in advance. Here are some of the more common questions that are usually part of a traditional interview:

- Tell us a little about yourself. (Ninety-five percent of all traditional interviews begin this way.)

- What are your strengths and weaknesses?

- What do you hope to be doing five years from now?

- What are your long-term goals and objectives?

- Why did you choose this particular career path?

- Why are you interested in working with us?

- What is your greatest professional accomplishment to date, and your greatest professional disappointment?

And my all-time favorite:

- If you were a tree, what kind of tree would you be?

The traditional interview has always bothered me. Interviewers too often surrender control of the interview to the applicant, which is absurd. Moreover, interviewers seem resolutely determined to ask the kinds of questions that can easily be anticipated by candidates, many of whom have rehearsed their answers.

Then, too, there's the matter of honesty. Using the traditional inter-view format, there's absolutely no way of knowing whether a candi-date is telling the truth or engaging in pure fantasy. Furthermore, the traditional interview offers the candidate who's well rehearsed or pro-ficient in the art of interviewing a tailor-made opportunity to eclipse those who are better qualified for the position.

But the most irritating part of the traditional interview is the contribu-tion it makes to poor hiring decisions. Because interviews of this type often lack substance, "gut feelings" frequently replace solid, objective judgements based on a candidate's strengths and competencies. Too often, the subjective information derived from the interview is used only to support and reinforce decisions based on "gut feelings."

CAUTION

> Never confuse the quality of an interview with the qual-ity of a candidate. A good interviewer seeks to match the skills and competencies of an applicant with the manda-tory success factors of the job; a good candidate is one who closely matches what is being sought. A candidate with great interviewing skills is not necessarily a great candidate for the job.

Interviewers sometimes attempt to "structure" the traditional interview—ask the same prepared questions of every candidate—especially for civil service positions. While structuring the traditional interview may prevent claims of unfair hiring practices by unsuccessful applicants, they do little to solve the real problem of figuring out who's best for the job. The kinds of questions asked in the typical traditional interview usually result in hiring decisions based on unreliable and highly subjective information. And most attempts at structuring don't even include a uniform method of evaluating candidates based upon the job's mandatory success factors.

PLAIN ENGLISH

Unstructured interview   An informal process similar to a conversation with an applicant. In unstructured interviews, the interviewer asks questions about key areas of concern that may be different for each applicant. In a structured interview process, questions specifically relating to an open position are formulated in advance of the interview and each question is asked of each applicant. Structured interviews are more formal.

Advantages: The traditional interview provides an opportunity to engage in a rapport-building exercise that may be enjoyable.

Disadvantages: Numerous. In my opinion, the traditional interview, and the poor hiring decisions that it inspires, is a surefire way for an organization to guarantee itself a high percentage of hiring mistakes. The fact is, the traditional interview no longer works, and probably never did.

STRESS INTERVIEW

"Do you see this paper clip I'm holding in my hand? Paper clips are useful little tools, wouldn't you agree? Tell me 12 uses for a paper clip. You have 60 seconds, beginning now."

The role of an interviewer drastically changes in a stress interview. The interviewer becomes more of an interrogator who deliberately asks questions designed to make an applicant feel uncomfortable and insecure.

The purpose of stress interviews is to discover whether a candidate can cope with difficult, demanding situations in which the best in performance is required even in the worst of conditions. Some jobs, after all, not only necessitate someone with the technical expertise to do the job, but also someone who can keep cool even in incredibly stressful situations.

TIP

> Stress interviews have their place, but only in situations in which the position being sought is extremely demanding. Even then, a stress interview should be used only as a follow-up to the primary interview, and only finalists should be invited to participate.

Questions asked of candidates in a stress interview can often sound crude and offensive. They're designed to be. Questions are phrased to determine whether a candidate will react to the sarcasm and general nastiness of the interviewer, or maintain a sense of restraint and deal with questions in a noncombative manner. Will the candidate lose composure or maintain it in the midst of a stressful environment?

Stress interviews are justified when job-related questions like these need to be answered:

- Can the candidate survive the rigors of being part of a special services police unit where life and death situations are routine, or will the candidate come unglued and place his life and the lives of others in jeopardy?

- Can the candidate handle the extreme daily pressures of being an air traffic controller responsible for the lives and safety of unnumbered air travelers together with multiple millions of dollars in equipment?

- Will the candidate succumb to the strain of a large city newspaper where work is regularly done under the pressure of surrealistically compressed deadlines?

For these and similar occupations, a stress interview may well be an important part of the selection process.

Advantages: Stress interviews, although unpleasant for the candidate and the interviewer, are an effective method of determining whether a candidate can function professionally under extreme conditions.

Disadvantages: While stress interviews may help determine an applicant's ability to work under extreme conditions, it's important to
remember that those with some rather severe types of personality disorders will also do well. Also, overly zealous interviewers can chase
off all but the most confrontational (and therefore potentially unman-
ageable) candidates.

TEAM INTERVIEW

"As you know, it's our unit's job to publish the monthly company
newsletter. Tell us what publications experience you've had in your
present and former jobs."

Team interviews are becoming increasingly popular. They operate on
the premise that the more knowledgeable people who are involved in
the hiring process, the better the hiring decision will be.

Using the team interview approach, selected members of a division,
department, or unit where the job opening exists meet with the candidate either individually or as a group. Each team member is free to
ask the candidate job-related questions.

Following the interview, team members discuss the candidate's
strengths and weaknesses in relationship to the job and record their
impressions.

Team interviews can be effective, but only when they're structured (all
applicants are asked the same job-related questions) and team members use a common assessment guide to rate applicants. Unstructured
interviewing by teams often degenerates into group conversations,
with the hiring decision being based on "gut instinct."

Advantages: Team interviews involve people with a vested interest in
selecting the right candidate for the job. After all, they are the people
with whom the successful candidate will eventually work. An additional
advantage is that employees are more committed to helping a new-
comer succeed when they have had direct input in the hiring decision.

Disadvantages: Teams sometimes resist structure and, in doing so,
destroy the real value of team interviews.

TIP

Team interviews work best when they are part of another interview format. For example, a team approach to interviewing candidates using the structured behavioral model (discussed later in this lesson) will maintain the advantages of team interviewing and include the structure and evaluation tools necessary to maintain objectivity.

SITUATIONAL INTERVIEW

"Suppose on your first day at work with us the telephone rings. It's a call from an irate customer who is threatening to sue us unless we take back the equipment he bought from us and refund his money. What would you do?"

The situational interview is similar to a traditional interview, with some important differences. The situational interview is usually structured and makes use of a common assessment guide.

Questions are *hypothetical* and designed to elicit responses that provide a glimpse into a candidate's thinking processes, personal values, creativity, and practical experience.

PLAIN ENGLISH

Hypothetical   Imaginary. Hypothetical interview questions attempt to discover how a candidate would act if a certain situation were to occur; both the question and the response are purely conjecture.

Hypothetical problems can also be given to candidates to analyze and solve as the interviewer (or interview team) looks on. This presents the opportunity to evaluate candidates as they attempt to solve problems that may actually occur on the job. Is the candidate completely befuddled by the problem? Has the candidate plunged headfirst into the problem only to offer a quick, simplistic solution? In wrestling with the problem, does the candidate demonstrate exceptional problem-solving skills, including analyzing and strategizing a solution? Does the candidate offer reasoned responses that display a unique combination of imagination, courage, and creativity?

The fundamental problem with the situational interview is that it deals only with the hypothetical. You can't assume that a candidate will be a highly creative problem solver on the job just because he or she solved a hypothetical problem in an interview.

Without a doubt, situational interviews provide some insight into the way a candidate thinks, feels, and acts. But they don't provide you with the objective information necessary to help you make an informed hiring decision. For example, one of the most critical deficiencies of the situational interview is that you learn what a candidate *could do* in the hypothetical situation being discussed, instead of what that person *has done* in different but similarly challenging situations in the past.

Advantages: Situational interviews provide some insight into a candidate's problem-solving skills, reasoning abilities, and creativity. They are interesting for the interviewer, and challenging for the candidate.

Disadvantages: By concentrating on the hypothetical, the interviewer never learns about how a candidate has actually behaved in the past when confronted with different but similarly challenging situations. Hypothetical solutions to hypothetical problems force a candidate to offer only conjecture about what could be done.

STRUCTURED BEHAVIORAL INTERVIEW

"Tell me about a time when you disagreed with a decision made by your boss. What did you do?"

Structured behavioral interviewing is based on this simple premise: The most accurate predictor of future performance is past performance in a similar situation. This form of interviewing focuses on real-life job-related experiences, behaviors, knowledge, skills, and abilities.

Candidates are asked to talk about actual situations in which they've had to use certain skills and abilities. In answering behavioral questions, candidates draw from their past experiences at work, in school, as a volunteer, or even from extracurricular activities and hobbies. Structured behavioral interviewing is considered a modern business best practice.

In Lesson 6, "Structured Behavioral Interviewing: Part 1," we'll discuss structured behavioral interviewing at length. But for the purposes of this lesson, it's important to understand that structured behavioral interviewing can revolutionize your interviewing practices and, according to my research, improve your chances of hiring the right candidates by as much as 300 percent.

Advantages: Structured behavioral interviewing enables you to catch a glimpse of a candidate dealing with real-life situations that required the same skills and abilities that your open position requires. A structured behavioral format allows you to get "behind" the resumé and explore the depth and breadth of a candidate's experience and training. Job-related questions are prepared in advance, and the same questions are asked of each candidate interviewed. Combined with a rating system tied to the mandatory success factors that you're seeking, this model is an objective and highly effective way to select a candidate.

Disadvantages: Initially, adjusting to the structured behavioral model can be challenging, especially for those who have used the traditional interview model for years. With a little practice, however, you'll soon be comfortable with structured behavioral interviewing.

THE 30-SECOND RECAP

- Selecting the best format for an employment interview is one of the most important tasks in the selection process.

- Telephone interviews are an effective and inexpensive way to help narrow the field of candidates to a manageable number.

- The traditional interview usually results in traditionally high numbers of hiring mistakes.

- Stress interviews should be reserved for positions that involve extremely stressful conditions.

- Team interviews work well when they are part of a structured interview format.

- Situational interviews deal in the hypothetical; candidates offer conjecture about what they might do in a given situation.

- Structured behavioral interviews focus on the behavior of candidates in past situations requiring skills and abilities similar to those required by the position they're interviewing for.

LESSON 6
Structured Behavioral Interviewing: Part 1

In this lesson, you learn about structured behavioral interviewing and how a typical structured behavioral interview works.

WHY STRUCTURED BEHAVIORAL INTERVIEWING?

Whether you're searching for an entry-level employee or a seasoned executive, structured behavioral interviewing will help you select the best candidate for the job. The technique is based on the *behavioral consistency principle* that the best method of predicting future behavior is to determine past behavior under similar circumstances.

PLAIN ENGLISH

> **Behavioral Consistency Principle**   Argues that the best predictor of future behavior is past behavior in similar situations.

Practically speaking, the behavioral consistency principle suggests that probes such as "Tell me about a disagreement you've had with your boss" will prompt more worthwhile information about an applicant than questions such as "If you were a tree, what kind of tree would you be?"

Behavioral questions force candidates to discuss real-life situations in which they use key skills to solve problems. As a result, interviewers are given a unique opportunity to look "behind" the resumé and discover a candidate's real potential.

TIP

> Expect some candidates—those who rehearsed their answers in preparation for a traditional interview—to be surprised that the questions you ask require them to think and reveal real-life behaviors.

Structured behavioral interviewing has a proven track record of success. My informal research has shown that this method of interviewing improves the probability of hiring successfully by more than three times the rate of a traditional, less structured interview. Current employment literature reports similar findings and recommends structured behavioral interviewing as a best practice.

But that's not all. Consider these added benefits:

- Structured behavioral interviewing provides an orderly, efficient process of job-related assessment.

- Behaviorally based questions yield more valuable information about a candidate than questions normally asked in traditional interviews.

- Managers obtain and evaluate behavioral evidence of skills and abilities before making critical hiring decisions.

- Legal guidelines involving fairness in the selection process are respected.

- There is maximum assurance that a good match will ultimately exist between new hires and the jobs that they enter.

- Structured behavioral interviewing results in shorter new employee training time, higher initial productivity, and significantly lower rates of turnover.

Successful organizations use structured behavioral interviewing because it works. Hiring decisions based on behavioral evidence about a candidate's job-related skills are bound to be better decisions than those based on a "hunch" or "a gut feeling."

HOW STRUCTURED BEHAVIORAL INTERVIEWING IS DIFFERENT

Traditional forms of interviewing can enable some candidates to look good because they offer the ideal opportunity to display their presentation skills and knowledge of the subject matter. But talking in generalizations is one thing, and offering concrete examples is another.

Structured behavioral interviewing requires a candidate to talk about real-life situations in which they used the particular skill being evaluated. Using the structured behavioral interview model, it's not "Do you know how to do it?" but rather "Tell us how you've done it and the result that you achieved."

Structured behavioral interviews differ from traditional interview formats in a number of additional important ways. For example:

- Control of the structured behavioral interview always remains with the interviewer. Candidates are never allowed to redirect the focus of questions to areas of their own choosing.

- The interview is "structured," which means that the same job-related questions are asked of all candidates and that each question is based on a specific mandatory success factor of the job.

- Candidates are evaluated using a standard evaluation tool also based on mandatory success factors. "Gut feelings" and "hunches" are ignored.

- Candidates are not presented with hypothetical questions to answer or problems to solve. Instead of being asked to speculate on what they would do in certain situations, candidates are asked what they have actually done in similar situations in the past.

- Follow-up probes, similar to those used in more traditional types of interviewing, are used extensively to test answers for accuracy, honesty, and consistency.

- Interviewers take copious notes throughout the interview, as opposed to other forms of interviewing, in which taking notes is not as much of a priority.

A CONSISTENT INTERVIEW PROCESS

Consistency is important in the interview process. It ensures that interviewers perform quality interviews that elicit relevant information, and that candidates leave with a favorable impression of the organization.

The structured behavioral interview process is no exception. You'll need to consider the following consistency guidelines.

First, if you plan to use a panel of interviewers, be careful whom you select. This is especially important if the position being filled is a senior position. For most positions, however, a good rule of thumb is to invite all supervisors to whom the new employee will report, together with a peer or two from the department or unit in which the opening exists. These are the people who know what it takes to get the job done; their input will be valuable.

TIP

> A panel interview offers the advantage of allowing several interviewers to question and evaluate a candidate. Consider assigning roles to members of the interview team: "hostile interviewer," "friendly interviewer," "company salesman," and so on. How a candidate responds to the various personalities can in itself be revealing.

Second, in developing the interview process, make sure that you allocate enough time for each interview, remembering that part of the time allotted must be devoted to evaluating the candidate following the interview. Usually the position to be filled will determine the length of the interview. (It's common for middle-management positions to require interview slots of two hours or more.) Don't short-change either the candidate or yourself by failing to provide an appropriate amount of time for the tasks to be accomplished.

Third, be sure to stay on schedule. Nothing communicates unprofessionalism quicker than interviews that always seem to be "running late." Start on time; end on time. In fact, it's a good idea to inform a candidate of an anticipated end time before the interview begins. Concern about time demonstrates regard for the candidate and for those participating in the interview.

Fourth, to the extent possible, arrange only morning interviews. It's a fact that neither candidate nor interviewer performs as well later in the afternoon. Give yourself and your candidates an opportunity to perform at peak levels.

Finally, try to avoid interviewing more than two to three candidates a day. It's difficult to do justice to more than that.

PLAN EACH STAGE OF THE INTERVIEW

To ensure consistency in the interview process, be sure that your interviews contain three major parts:

- Opening
- Information exchange
- Closing

Although each stage is distinct and has a unique purpose, the overall process should be seamless. Moving from the opening to the information exchange and finally to the closing should be done smoothly and naturally.

TIP

> Give each interviewer all the candidate's information well in advance of the interview. This will enable each participant to ask pertinent questions about a candidate's background, and generally will enhance the interviewer's ability to evaluate candidates.

THE OPENING

Interviews should open with a genuine attempt to put the candidate at ease. The interviewer (or primary interviewer, in panel interview formats) should use body language that conveys warmth and genuine pleasure in meeting the candidate—standing when the candidate enters the room, leaning forward to offer a handshake, and smiling are great ways to break the ice and establish instant positive rapport.

Once the candidate is seated, introduce him or her to everyone participating in the interview and ask each panel member to introduce themselves by name and position within the organization.

The opening of the interview is the time to talk about the interview process. Tell the candidate what to expect during the interview.

Begin by providing a context for the interview. You might say something like, "The purpose of our interview with you today is to provide you with an opportunity to learn more about our organization ... and for us to learn more about you. We're particularly interested in learning whether you have the qualifications we're seeking for the position of sales manager."

CAUTION

> In attempting to help a candidate feel at ease, it's tempting to ask a few personal questions that are irrelevant to the job. Resist the temptation! Even innocent questions about a candidate's family are prohibited and could be grounds for a discrimination action by an unsuccessful applicant.

THE INFORMATION EXCHANGE

The information exchange is the central part of the interview. During the information exchange, questions are asked and information is received that will lead directly to a decision to hire or not to hire. Don't hesitate to ask as many follow-up questions as needed whenever you feel that more information is required.

Be sure that all questions about the candidate's experience, education, and work history are asked and answered. Now is the time to explore any gaps in a candidate's employment history, and to confirm (if necessary) important information about education, experience, and job-related skills and abilities. Such questions should be limited; this is not a time to ask a candidate to make a verbal presentation of the entire resumé.

TIP

Practice the 80/20 rule: During the core part of an interview, the candidate should do 80 percent of the talking, and the interviewer should do only 20 percent. Resist the urge to help candidates who become stalled or who are searching for words to convey information.

To help put a candidate at ease, it's wise to ask easier questions first. Questions about the candidate's resumé or application having to do with experience or training work particularly well in the beginning of an interview, as do questions that elicit insight into a candidate's character and personality such as, "Of all the jobs you've held in the past, which was the one you liked best and why?"

As you move into the more difficult structured behavioral questions, be sure to allow the candidate time to think through each question and formulate a response. Allow periods of silence. Don't rush the candidate, either verbally or nonverbally.

CLOSING

The manner in which you close an interview will leave a lasting impression on the candidate. Interviews should be closed in a professional, unhurried manner. Ask one member of the team to "sell the company" by presenting the benefits of working for the organization and the opportunities that exist. Invite the candidate to ask any lingering questions. Finally, tie up any loose ends that need attention, and inform the candidate of what to expect next.

Don't forget to thank the candidate for participating in the interview. By standing and offering a handshake, you signal to the candidate that the interview has concluded.

A CONSISTENT EVALUATION PROCESS

In the structured behavioral interview model, the process of evaluating candidates should also be structured. You should devise an assessment tool to help your organization evaluate candidates consistently. (See Appendix B, "Interview Evaluation Summary.")

THE ASSESSMENT TOOL

Design your assessment tool with simplicity and consistency in mind. The idea is to assess a candidate's behavioral evidence as it relates to the mandatory success factors required by the position. That's as technical as your tool should get.

TIP

> Occasionally I've found assessment tools that appear to be very complicated and technical. With some of them, the math alone would probably frighten Einstein. Take my word for it, you don't need anything that complicated. I recommend that you construct your own assessment tool and keep it simple. Simple tools are usually the most effective.

In constructing an assessment tool, devise a system in which mandatory success factors identified within each skill set are weighted depending on importance. For example, if there are six mandatory success factors in the technical skills set, the most important of the six factors would be given a weight of 6; the second most important would be weighted 5; the third would be weighted 4; and so on.

Candidate performance scores for each factor, which may range from 0 (poor) to 5 (excellent), are then multiplied by the weight factor to arrive at an adjusted score for the factor being assessed. If several members of an interview team have rated the candidate, average the scores for each skill set to determine final candidate scores (see Appendix B).

SOME ADDITIONAL IDEAS TO CONSIDER

Here are some additional ideas to consider as you develop a process for evaluating candidates following an interview:

- Don't wait. Make it a point to take a few minutes following each interview to complete the evaluation. The quality of evaluations sharply decreases when they are completed following a series of interviews.

- If you have used a panel of interviewers, hold off any discussion of a candidate's strengths and weaknesses until each member has completed the written evaluation.

- Instruct each team participant to focus on the evidence of important job-related skills. Don't allow "gut feelings" to play a role in the evaluation process.

- Be sure that all interviewer notes have to do with a job-related topic. Ignore anything that is not directly applicable to the job for which the candidate has applied.

- Make sure that interviewer notes are legible and that they contain complete sentences. Interviewer notes may become very important when it's time to make a hiring decision.

Location of the Interview

Deciding on a location for the interview is an important part of the planning process. Choose a location suitable to the situation.

For example, if the position you're attempting to fill is, at the moment, confidential, choose a location away from the office. Private meeting rooms in hotels can work well in these instances.

But most of the time, candidates are interviewed in the workplace. For those situations, I recommend conducting interviews in an office or meeting room that is comfortable, well lit, and free of disrupting noise. Your objective should be an atmosphere that will help the candidate feel at ease.

If there's a telephone in the room, unplug it or turn off the ringer. Consider hanging a "Do Not Disturb" sign on the door during the interview to prevent unnecessary interruptions. Instruct members of the interview panel to turn off cellular phones and pagers. Advise secretaries and other office staff to disturb panel members only in cases of extreme emergency.

Also be mindful of seating arrangements. Panel interviews are sometimes set up so that the candidate, sitting alone, faces the interview panel, seated at a long table. This can be a very intimidating arrangement for the candidate (although effective if you want to observe a candidate's behavior in a tense situation). A less intimidating arrangement would be for the interview panel to be seated around a long table, with the candidate at one end.

CAUTION

Make sure that the candidate's chair is not lower than the chairs used by the panel members. Otherwise, the candidate may be intimidated unintentionally.

THE 30-SECOND RECAP

- Structured behavioral interviewing is based on the theory that the best predictor of future behavior is past behavior in similar circumstances.

- Structured behavioral interviewing examines behavioral evidence of a candidate's skills and abilities, and compares them to identified mandatory success factors of the job being sought.

- The process of structured behavioral interviewing should be well defined and communicated to all who participate so that interviews are conducted in a consistent manner.

- The primary purpose of the interview is to hear from the candidate, so be sure to follow the 80/20 rule—let the candidate do most of the talking.

- Scoring by evaluators should be completed immediately following each interview to preserve integrity of the data and to maintain consistency.

- Make location and seating arrangements part of your interview planning process.

LESSON 7

Structured Behavioral Interviewing: Part 2

In this lesson, you learn how to develop effective behavioral questions and follow-up probes *that get behind the resumé to explore a candidate's competency in key areas.*

LEARNING TO ASK QUESTIONS

Structured behavioral interviewing is designed to minimize personal impressions and focus instead on a candidate's actions and behaviors. That's important because successful hiring decisions are based on objective behavioral evidence demonstrating a candidate's proficiency with identified job-related skills—not on subjective impressions.

Learning to develop questions that explore a candidate's past behaviors is key. Become proficient at it, and your "successful hire" numbers will start to skyrocket.

QUESTIONING CONSISTENTLY

One reason that structured behavioral interviewing is so effective is its use of consistent questions. You achieve consistency when you ask the same behavioral questions of each candidate and align each question to a mandatory success factor within a specific skill set.

Whether you're interviewing for chief executive officer or custodian, these are the skill sets that you'll want to consider:

> **CAUTION**
>
> In developing questions and follow-up probes, remember to keep them focused on the mandatory success factors of the job being sought. As tempting as it may be to wander into more personal areas, avoid doing so. Seeking information unrelated to the job is looking for trouble.

- Technical skills (or competencies)
- Functional skills
- Self-management skills
- Interpersonal skills

In Lesson 1, "Analyzing the Position," we discussed the importance of analyzing a job to identify mandatory success factors for each of the skill sets. Once identified, mandatory success factors are weighted by order of importance, and behavioral questions are developed for each factor.

The objective is to discover behavioral evidence of a candidate's level of competency in each of the skills required for success. Follow-up probes are used to ensure that each key skill has been thoroughly explored, and to confirm information or challenge inconsistencies.

DEVELOPING BEHAVIORAL QUESTIONS

Behavioral questions seek responses from candidates based on their real-life work experiences. Each response should demonstrate the practical use of key skills and abilities necessary for success in the job under consideration.

Asking each candidate the same behavioral questions ensures fairness and consistency in the interview process. But more than that, the procedure provides a fair and equitable means of objectively comparing each candidate's qualifications—and protects you from charges of illegal hiring practices.

OPEN BEHAVIORAL QUESTIONS

Prepare *open behavioral questions* for all identified mandatory success factors. Their purpose is to reveal key behavioral information by encouraging a candidate to talk about past situations in which the use of a particular skill was important.

PLAIN ENGLISH

Open behavioral questions   Questions that cannot be answered with a simple "yes" or "no." They require a candidate to discuss at length an incident from the past that required a working knowledge of specific skills.

Because open behavioral questions seek descriptions of real-life personal and interpersonal situations, they usually begin with phrases such as these:

- "Tell me about ..."
- "Describe a time when you ..."
- "Give me an example of a time in which you ..."
- "Describe the most significant ..."
- "What did you do in your last job when ..."
- "Describe a situation in which you ..."
- "Relate a personal story in which you ..."
- "Relate a scenario where you ..."
- "Narrate a situation in school when you ..."

- "Describe an opportunity in which you ..."

- "Tell me about an occasion in which you ..."

TIP

> Don't worry about silences during the interview, when candidates attempt to think of appropriate behavioral responses to questions. Your questions are not only causing them to think, but to openly discuss areas that may be sensitive.

Occasionally a candidate will have to be prompted to provide more information about a disclosed situation or problem. You can accomplish this by using additional open probes such as these:

- "Oh?"

- "Tell me more."

- "Really?"

- "Please go on."

- "What happened then?"

- "I'd be interested in knowing more about that."

Probes such as these not only encourage a candidate to provide more information, but they also offer assurance that you're listening and interested in what's being said.

TIP

> Structured behavioral interviewing is not designed to find a candidate with "all the right answers." In fact, the ideal candidate should be one who demonstrates a steady growth in competence and skill over time. Candidates who are courageous enough to reveal behavior that they now recognize to be faulty demonstrate growth and maturity.

FOLLOW-UP PROBES

Follow-up probes can be either open or closed, depending on the information that you seek. Open follow-up probes are used to search for further behavioral evidence of a skill, to provide more information about a specific event, or to resolve inconsistencies. Open follow-up probes can also be used to guide a wandering candidate back to the question at hand.

Because they are responsive to information provided by a candidate, open follow-up probes are always impromptu and usually begin with one of these phrases:

- "Tell me more about ..."
- "Help me to understand why ..."
- "Could you explain ..."
- "I'd be interested in hearing more about ..."
- "Let's talk more about ..."
- "I'd like to return to my original question, which is ..."

Closed follow-up probes are used to solicit very specific information. This kind of probe can usually be answered with a "yes" or "no" or with just a few words. Closed follow-up probes are used to obtain confirmation of important information or to clear up misunderstandings. Here are a few examples of closed follow-up probes:

- "You said that you have fully qualified for a state license to practice acupuncture?"
- "Did I hear you say that you think your present employer is a crook?"
- "Is it correct that you graduated from Dartmouth in June of 1992?"
- "When do you expect to take your CPA examination?"

Example of an Open Behavioral Question with Open Follow-Up Probes

"Tell me about a time when you were completely over your head with work on a particular project. How did you deal with the situation?"

The purpose of the question is to assess the candidate's ability to manage time. This question would be asked if being skilled in time management was one of the identified mandatory success factors.

Follow-up probes could include questions such as these:

- "That's interesting. Tell me more about what you did to get control of the situation."

- "How did you decide which task to do first?"

- "What was the outcome of your actions?"

- "What could you have done differently?"

- "How did the experience change the way you work today?"

Note that the purpose of each of these open follow-up probes is to more fully explore the candidate's personal thoughts, feelings, motivations, and behavior. Questions that begin with "why," "what," or "how" accomplish this objective particularly well.

Use open follow-up probes freely. In fact, it's helpful to continue to probe until you've discovered the result of a given action or learned how the situation turned out. And in some cases, it's entirely appropriate to ask the candidate what could have been done differently or better.

Candidates Who Lie

Occasionally follow-up probes make it plain that a candidate is not providing truthful behavioral information at all. ("You indicated in your answer that you began your research project in April of 1994; your resumé, however, indicates that during that period you were a full-time student. Could you please explain further?") Confronted with behavioral questioning, candidates sometimes attempt to fabricate stories rather than to discuss real-life situations. On catching a candidate in a lie, some interviewers politely end the interview and disqualify the candidate from further consideration.

How you handle a deceitful candidate is up to you. But if you elect to continue to interview a candidate who has been untruthful, at the very least make careful note of the situation so that the matter is taken into account in the evaluation phase of the process. Telling boldfaced lies in an interview reveals much about a candidate's character and sense of personal integrity. This kind of information should not be ignored.

CAUTION

> Don't conclude that a candidate has lied to you unless the candidate actually confirms the falsehood. Unless confirmed by the candidate, opinions in this regard are dangerous and should not appear in the notes of the interview.

CONTRARY EVIDENCE QUESTIONS

At first, this type of question seems tricky and may feel uncomfortable to ask. But the intent of contrary evidence questions is not to trick or trap a candidate, but to drill down to reveal what's behind a candidate's past work experiences. Contrary evidence questions are an effective tool to use in exploring the degree and refinement of a candidate's skills.

Contrary evidence questions have two parts: the first part describes a situation that is somewhat negative; the second part asks for behavioral evidence that demonstrates action taken by the candidate that was contrary to the precipitating situation. The second part of the question is asked only after the first part has been answered. For example:

Interviewer: "What things make you angry?"

After candidates answer the question by telling the interviewer all the things that make them angry, the second part of the question is then asked:

Interviewer: "How do you deal with each of those situations?"

Here are a few more contrary evidence questions to consider:

- "Tell me about a time when you had to make a difficult decision about a matter that wasn't covered by a company policy. What did you do?"

- "Do you have job-related areas that you need to improve? Tell me about a time that illustrates your need for improvement."

- "What experience have you had dealing with subordinates with performance problems? Give me an example of a recent problem and how you resolved it."

- "What were the major obstacles that you encountered in your present job? Tell me how you overcame each of them."

At least one contrary evidence question should be included in every structured behavioral interview. The ability to positively impact negative situations is of vital importance. Questions that begin with behavioral negatives tend to take candidates off guard a bit, but result in excellent behavioral evidence that is very valuable.

CONTINUUM QUESTIONS

Another kind of question that provides valuable insight is the continuum question. Continuum questions place candidates between two positive qualities, one of which is an identified mandatory success factor and critical to the successful performance of the job being sought, the other of which is something that may be a commendable skill but not a mandatory success factor for the position.

Here are some examples of effective continuum questions (remember to ask for specific behavioral evidence for the answer):

- "On a continuum between being a team player and working independently, where do you see yourself?"
- "On a continuum between being a loner and being a people person, where do you fit?"
- "On a continuum between hating new technology and loving it, where do you fit?"

Try using a continuum question to explore areas of personal preference. Use follow-up questions to explore responses thoroughly, and don't be afraid to ask for behavioral evidence for the answers provided.

SELF-APPRAISAL QUESTIONS

Self-appraisal questions present an opportunity to learn how candidates think others perceive them. Make an effort to include a self-appraisal question in every interview. The question asks a candidate to evaluate how others perceive his or her performance of a mandatory success factor. This can be very revealing.

Here's a typical self-appraisal question:

"If I were to call your present supervisor, how would she describe your ability to meet deadlines on a timely basis?"

And here's a bonus for those who followed my earlier recommendation and already talked with the candidate's supervisor: You'll immediately be able to compare a candidate's response with the actual report of the supervisor. The supervisor may have also provided enough additional information about the candidate's work experience to know whether a more thorough assessment of other key areas is warranted.

But whether you contact references before an interview or afterward, the self-appraisal question is a valuable tool. It will help you assess whether there's congruity in the way candidates think they are perceived, and the way they're actually perceived by those who have supervised them and know them well. Lack of congruity in this regard could mean that the candidate may be out-of-touch with reality in some important way or simply attempting to mislead the interviewer.

Be sure to use follow-up probes to obtain behavioral evidence for a candidate's answer. "Why," "what," and "how" probes will help provide the necessary additional information. Be prepared to learn some interesting and useful information about a candidate using this style of question.

ANSWERING BEHAVIORAL QUESTIONS: THE STAR FORMULA

TIP

> Some candidates may lack on-the-job experience. In those instances, ask behavioral questions that explore real life experiences from school or from volunteer service. Behavioral evidence of skills used in these settings is also a valid indicator of a candidate's likelihood of success on the job.

Behavioral questions are intended to make candidates think. Responses should tell a complete story with a beginning, a middle, and an end. You should expect stories of this nature to convey a considerable amount of factual detail. In fact, it's the lack of detail that often betrays those who attempt to fabricate behavioral stories.

I recommend using the STAR technique to ensure that a candidate's story is fully probed. Here's how the STAR technique works:

- **S and T = situation or task** A candidate should talk about a specific situation or task in which they had to use certain skills and abilities to deal with a real problem or concern.

- **A = action** Find out what actions the candidate took to resolve the situation or perform the task. Actions are important because they reveal the extent of the candidate's ability to use many of the skills required in a new employee. This area requires thorough exploration through the use of follow-up probes.

- **R = results**   Don't forget to find out the result of the candidate's actions. Were the results those that were intended? What could the candidate have done differently or better?

This simple formula will help you explore behavioral situations completely and obtain valuable information about a candidate's ability to use key skills in practical ways. The formula also helps keep interviews focused and on track.

TIP

> Limit your interviews to the very best candidates. Also limit the number of candidates (six to eight is optimal) who will be offered an interview. Remember, the shorter the short list, the quicker you'll be able to fill the position.

SECOND INTERVIEW STRATEGIES

Sometimes, depending on the position, the first round of interviews will result in the selection of candidates for a *short list*. That means that a second interview eventually needs to take place.

But second interviews can be quite different from the first. A number of strategies work well for second interviews. Each of these strategies attempts to further evaluate a candidate's qualifications by having the candidate become involved in some form of actual work experience.

PLAIN ENGLISH

> **Short list**   A list of a few select candidates who achieved the highest scores in an initial interview and have been chosen to continue with the selection process.

PROJECT REVIEW

In this method of evaluation, candidate finalists are assigned projects. For consistency and fairness, each candidate is assigned the same project.

Projects should require specific criteria and should be based on the job being sought. For example, candidates for a sales manager position might be asked to present a plan for keeping the sales staff motivated. Candidates for a marketing manager position might be asked to develop a strategic marketing plan for a specific product or service.

Assignments have deadlines, and project review assignments are no exception. Candidates usually are allowed no more than two or three days to complete the task. When projects are completed, a second interview is scheduled in which candidates present their work and answer questions from the interview panel. Candidates are evaluated based on the quality and content of their presentations, and the final selection is then made.

ON-THE-JOB TRIAL

The on-the-job trial is a strategy that seems to be increasing in popularity. It offers employers an opportunity to observe a candidate as a functioning part of the unit, department, or division in which the job opening exists.

Candidates are invited to spend a day on the job with various members of the interview panel. During the day, the candidate is asked to perform specific tasks that relate to the highest-rated mandatory success factors.

Observers rate each candidate on demonstrated skill proficiency. But equally important are observations about the manner in which candidates relate to members of the panel and to those with whom they would be working.

The Situational Problem

The situational problem is an interesting variation on the project review model. Instead of a project, a candidate is assigned a situational problem to solve. Problems are usually complex, requiring several issues to be addressed.

Candidates are asked to solve the situational problem by doing all the things necessary to achieve a favorable result. Candidates may have to write letters or internal memoranda, hold staff meetings, convene brainstorming sessions, or even conduct independent research. Consistency and fairness are maintained by giving the same problem to each of the candidates being evaluated.

Candidates submit their solutions within established deadlines, and their work is evaluated by members of the interview panel. This method of further candidate evaluation requires some planning, but the results are usually well worthwhile.

The 30-Second Recap

- Asking behavioral questions, which are linked to mandatory success factors, significantly improves your chances of hiring successfully.

- Use follow-up probes to seek further behavioral information.

- Use contrary evidence questions to explore the degree and refinement of a candidate's skills.

- Use continuum questions to explore areas of personal preference.

- Use self-appraisal questions to explore whether there's congruity in the way candidates think they are perceived, and the way they are actually perceived by others.

- Remember the STAR technique to guide candidates into providing complete answers to behavioral questions.

- When second interviews become necessary, consider the project review, on-the-job trial, and situational problem strategies.

Lesson 8
Controlling the Interview

In this lesson, you learn valuable techniques for maintaining control of the interview while obtaining the information that you need to evaluate candidates.

The Keys to Controlling the Interview

Effective interviews are focused, yielding important information about a candidate in a specified amount of time. Maintaining control of the interview is a vitally important task. Following are some valuable techniques that can help you stay in charge of the interview from beginning to end.

Preparation

Controlling the interview begins with the interviewer being well prepared. Preparation is essential to good interviewing. The more time you spend preparing, the more likely you'll hire successfully.

When preparing for an interview, don't skip any bases:

- Research the job thoroughly to identify mandatory success factors.

- Make copies of the current job description to provide candidates that you interview.

- Talk with previous jobholders and others who are familiar with the requirements of the job.

- Choose interview panel members who have a stake in finding the right person for the job.

- Structure the interview by developing position-specific questions that will be asked of all candidates and that correspond to mandatory success factors.

- Develop an evaluation tool to rate each candidate on the basis of behavioral responses to questions. See Appendix B, "Interview Evaluation Summary," for help.

REMEMBER THE 80/20 RULE

Don't forget the 80/20 rule. Let the candidate do 80 percent of the talking. The 20 percent of talking done by interviewers should be in the form of asking questions or using follow-up probes.

Many times during an interview you may feel tempted to abandon structured questions and simply converse with the candidate. Resist the urge. An interview (especially a behavioral interview) is not meant to be a casual conversation with a candidate. Its purpose is to obtain and assess specific behavioral information so that you can identify the best candidate for the job.

The 80/20 rule implies more for the interviewer than simply allowing candidates to do most of the talking. Interviewers should listen actively and intently to what a candidate says (and does not say) during the 80 percent of the time that they are not talking. Active listening provides you with a unique opportunity for insight into a candidate's behavioral patterns. Attentive listening also enables you to construct follow-up probes to further explore behavioral issues while keeping the interview on track. (See Lesson 10, "Active Listening Skills," for more on active listening.)

THE CLOCK IS RUNNING

During an interview, be mindful of the clock. Take responsibility for starting and ending on time and for accomplishing all that needs to be done during the course of the interview.

Don't let yourself run out of time or let the interview run long because you allowed candidates to respond to questions at length. Also avoid rushing through the last few questions because time is running out.

You provide adequate time for interviews by planning ahead. Estimate the time that candidates need to answer each set of behavioral questions and follow-up probes.

And don't forget to reserve time for evaluating the candidate after the interview has concluded. Both the candidate and the organization are shortchanged when evaluations are postponed to a later time.

PROBE IN DEPTH

Controlling the interview and obtaining the behavioral evidence that you need means following up each primary behavioral question with several follow-up probes.

Although it's true that some follow-up probes will be spontaneous, based on behavioral information provided by the candidate, you should develop several follow-up probes for each primary behavioral question before the interview.

Probe deeply to obtain all the behavioral evidence that's available. (See Lesson 7, "Structured Behavioral Interviewing; Part 2," for more information on effective probing techniques.)

SUPPORTIVE FEEDBACK

Use supportive feedback to calm and reassure candidates and to encourage sharing of important behavioral information. You should use supportive feedback throughout the interview, but it's particularly important early on, when the resumé-related exchange of information takes place. Helping the candidate to build confidence when easier questions are asked will pay off when the candidate is asked more sensitive questions.

Comments such as "That must have been very exciting for you" or "That must have been very difficult for you" provide the encouragement and support necessary for some candidates to talk freely.

Supportive feedback is important for every candidate, to be sure, but it's essential for the candidate who's nervous or distressed.

TIP

> The manner in which interviewers behave during an interview has a direct impact on a candidate. If a candidate displays nervousness, it's important for interviewers to remain calm and reassuring.

NONVERBAL ENCOURAGEMENT

As we've already discussed, in an ideal interview situation, the candidate speaks at least 80 percent of the time. It follows that during the course of an interview, interviewers will communicate with candidates in ways that are primarily nonverbal.

So just what is it that you want to communicate to candidates? Decide ahead of time. If your objective were to communicate skepticism and a certain degree of hostility, as in a stress interview, folding your arms and frowning while a candidate attempts to answer questions would convey the message. But if you're interested in encouraging a candidate freely and openly to provide behavioral evidence of his qualifications for the job, a much different nonverbal message is in order.

It's important to remember that nonverbal messaging begins before a candidate even enters the interview room. How a candidate is treated in waiting areas communicates much about the organization and the degree of importance that it places upon the position to be filled. Candidates who are ignored in waiting areas receive one message; those who are met with a smile and words of welcome, who are offered coffee or a soft drink, and whose arrival is immediately announced receive quite another message.

How a candidate is received in the interview room also conveys important messages about the organization and the open position. When the manager in charge meets the candidate at the door, extends a hand, smiles, and offers the candidate a seat, the message is one of warmth and welcome.

During the interview, smiles and nods from each member of the interview panel will also work wonders. Leaning forward in one's chair can also show interest in what's being said and offers significant nonverbal support.

An interviewer's nonverbal communication plays an important role in controlling the interview while simultaneously encouraging candidates to speak freely. Nonverbal communication is a powerful tool.

THE SOUNDS OF SILENCE

Interviewers sometimes panic during momentary silences in an interview. Big mistake. Just relax and let the silence happen.

Occasional lulls should be expected in every interview. Remember that structured behavioral interviewing requires the candidate to think. Thoughtful consideration requires silence.

Whatever you do, don't jump in to save a candidate with a follow-up question that attempts to make things easier or that changes the subject entirely. Instead, take the opportunity to observe how the candidate reacts to the additional stress.

Does the silence prompt the candidate to begin talking nervously to fill the void? Does the candidate try to change the subject? Does the candidate give up and confess his inability to answer the question? Or does the candidate use the silence to consider how best to answer the question? How a candidate reacts to silence can be revealing.

Momentary lulls do not mean that an interviewer has lost control of the interview. They are a natural part of the interview process. The interviewer loses control only when he or she panics and tries to fill the void.

TIP

Be careful how you act during silences. An interviewer who displays signs of obvious impatience will only add to the problem. Instead, reassure the candidate with comforting words, with a friendly smile, and with body language that conveys relaxation and acceptance. Remember, there's a difference between reassuring a candidate (in order to promote open communication) and jumping in to save a candidate by suggesting actions that might be taken, moving on to the next question quickly, and so forth.

MOVING ON

An interviewer's ability to keep the interview moving along is absolutely critical. But when should an interviewer move to the next question?

Use the STAR technique (see Lesson 7) to determine when you've thoroughly explored a behavioral situation and are ready to move on. Remember—every behavioral situation requires a number of actions; each action requires certain skills or competencies. Use follow-up probes to delve into each of these actions, the skills required to handle them, and, finally, what the result of each situation was.

Once you're satisfied that you have enough information about the specific competency to accurately assess the candidate's level of skill, move on! Whether the result was positive or negative, once you've used the STAR technique to probe it at length, you've accomplished your mission. Move on to the next question.

TIP

> What to do when you find yourself interviewing someone
> who is clearly underqualified for the position? Don't just
> go through the motions. Explain to the candidate that it
> appears that he or she simply doesn't have the work
> experience or skills that you're seeking. Thank the can-
> didate for his or her interest, and encourage the person
> to apply for other positions with your organizations in
> the future. Cut your losses early and move on!

THE NINE MOST COMMON MISTAKES INTERVIEWERS MAKE

Interviewing mistakes can be costly, especially if they result in the wrong candidate being hired. But the most common interviewing mistakes are entirely preventable. Knowing what they are is the first step in preventing them from occurring in your organization.

Here are the nine most common mistakes made by interviewers:

- Managers lack training in interviewing. Such lack of training can cause problems ranging from hiring the wrong person to being sued for asking illegal questions. Time, money, and effort invested in training managers to interview effectively pays immediate dividends and ensures quality hiring decisions.

- Interviewers fail to determine a position's mandatory success factors. If you haven't defined what it is that you need, how will you know it when you've found it?

- Panel members fail to prepare for interviews by meeting to discuss the process (discuss questions, decide who will ask what, etc.).

- Interview questions are not carefully prepared ahead of time, or they lack a behavioral component.

- The interview lacks depth as a result of inadequate follow-up probes designed to seek additional behavioral evidence.

- Interviewers surrender control of the interview to candidates who are skilled at interviewing and who redirect the course of the interview to areas that they're familiar with (and well-rehearsed in).

- In selecting candidates to interview, interviewers give little or no thought to the importance of diversity in the workplace.

- Interviewers compare candidates against each other instead of on the basis of mandatory success factors.

- Hiring decisions are made on the basis of "gut feelings," or "a twinkle in the eye," or "just a hunch."

Many of these mistakes may seem obvious, and they are. But as obvious as they are, they still occur. Avoid them, and you'll significantly increase your chances of hiring the right person for the job. Remember, it takes work to interview effectively, but the results are worth the effort.

Four Types of Candidate Responses and What They Mean

This chapter wouldn't be complete if it didn't include a brief section covering the four basic ways candidates respond to behavioral questions. To maintain control of the interview, you should be familiar with, and know how to react to, each.

Remember that a candidate will often employ more than one strategy during the course of an interview and can even attempt more than one strategy in answering a given question. Listen carefully for the type of response that the candidate uses, and react accordingly.

THE MOTOR MOUTH RESPONSE

The motor mouth response comes from a candidate who probably has little to say about a particular behavioral question. However, instead of pleading ignorance, this candidate attempts to gain control of the interview by talking incessantly. He or she hopes to redirect the interview to another topic of choice.

How to react: Try to gently bring the candidate back to the original question by using open probes. Failing that, don't hesitate to stop the candidate in mid-sentence, if necessary, and ask to return to the subject at hand. Sometimes it may be necessary to repeat the original question. Whatever you do, be sure to intervene. The motor mouth response is an attempt to impress the interviewer, but it's really a cover-up for a lack of competency. Don't be fooled by it.

THE SHORT STOP RESPONSE

This response is abrupt. The candidate answers a question with a short comment, sometimes consisting of just a few words, such as, "Whenever I had a problem, I'd ask my boss what to do, and then I did it." The interviewer, in an effort to draw the candidate out, uses follow-up probes that require a behavioral response with specific examples. But they, too, are met with terse responses. What's happening is that the candidate is extremely nervous, is attempting to hide something, or completely lacks the competency that you seek.

How to react: Use sufficient follow-up probes to be sure that you're dealing with a true short stop response and not just a nervous candidate. Once you're sure that you're dealing with a short stop, note the lack of responsiveness and move on to another question set dealing with the next mandatory success factor. If the pattern repeats itself, you may want to consider ending the interview. You're interested in obtaining behavioral evidence of key competencies; the candidate, for whatever reason, is interested in disclosing as little as possible. Proceeding further would likely be a waste of everyone's time.

THE GENERALIST RESPONSE

The generalist response is a clever attempt on the part of the candidate to cover up a real lack of competence. In fact, most of those who attempt a generalist response do so because the subject matter of the question is over their heads. Often, these are the candidates whose resumés contain a significant amount of "fluff."

The generalist response is similar to the motor mouth response in that candidates may opt to talk incessantly. However, unlike the motor mouth response, the generalist does not attempt to redirect the focus of the interview onto another topic. Instead, the generalist wants to provide general answers to specific questions.

For example, if asked, "Tell me about a time when your boss talked to you about a problem related to your work," the generalist might answer by talking at length about how employees in general can develop a positive working relationship with supervisors.

Often the information provided by a generalist response is quite good, and the candidate providing it may be very articulate. But notice how it misses the mark! The question in this example requires a specific behavioral response, not a general monologue on building rapport with one's supervisor. There's a big difference.

When pressed for specific behavioral evidence, candidates relying on the generalist response sometimes revert to providing interviewers with adjectives that describe how they see themselves in the situations being probed. For example, instead of providing behavioral evidence of being hardworking, a generalist response may be, "I'm a very hard-working person, and I always have been." But, again, note that the response is nonbehavioral and general.

How to react: Continue to press for behavioral evidence by using follow-up probes. If general responses continue, it sometimes helps to simply say, "But that's not what I asked. Let me restate my question." If after several attempts you still cannot make headway, summarize by saying, "I take it you have no examples you wish to share with us today." If after a few question sets the generalist response continues, consider ending the interview.

THE VALID RESPONSE

A valid response to a behavioral question or follow-up probe is a real-life account demonstrating how a candidate responded to a specific situation or task, together with an explanation of the actions taken and the results achieved (STAR). This response allows the interviewer to properly evaluate a candidate's level of competence with the success factor under consideration.

How to react: React by providing verbal and nonverbal support and encouragement. This is the kind of response that provides the information you need.

THE 30-SECOND RECAP

- Maintaining control over the interview is achievable by using a few simple techniques: prepare; remember the 80/20 rule; stay on time; probe in depth; use verbal and nonverbal supportive feedback; allow silence to happen; and, when it's appropriate, move on.

- There are nine common interview mistakes, each of which can be easily avoided.

- Candidates answer behavioral questions in four ways, each requiring an appropriate response by the interviewer.

LESSON 9
Navigating the Legal Minefield

In this lesson, you learn how to conduct a job interview without subjecting yourself and your organization to potential legal problems.

TAKING OFF THE BLINDFOLD

I'm always taken aback when I come across managers who haven't a clue about the legal aspects of interviewing. Interviewing without any knowledge of legalities is a little like insisting upon navigating a minefield blindfolded when the exact location of each mine has been marked with a big red flag.

The simple fact is that if you're going to be involved in the hiring process, you need to know where the legal mines have been planted. Their location has been well identified, but it's up to you to take off the blindfold and see them. Leave the blindfolds for the amateurs.

Remember that effective interviewing and legal interviewing are not mutually exclusive terms. It's both possible and desirable to plan interviews that not only are effective, but also avoid the legal pitfalls that abound.

> **CAUTION**
>
> Be advised that the author is not a practicing attorney, nor does he purport to give legal advice. Information concerning state and federal laws regulating employment practices as well as major court decisions is believed to be correct as of the date of publication. The law changes frequently, and every employment situation has its own unique legal concerns. Consult an employment attorney whenever questions arise, and review your organization's general hiring practices at regular intervals.

HIRING AND THE LAW

Numerous federal, state, and local equal opportunity and antidiscrimination laws regulate the application and interview process. Each of these laws was enacted to offer individuals and groups of protected persons legal protection against employment discrimination.

While state and local laws do not supersede federal legislation, they often are more restrictive or broader in scope. Managers must be aware of all laws affecting employment practices to prevent costly discrimination claims by unsuccessful applicants.

Here are just some of the federal laws that affect the hiring process:

- Title VII of the Civil Rights Act of 1964

- The Civil Rights Act of 1991

- The Americans with Disabilities Act

- The Immigration Reform Control Act of 1986

- Age Discrimination in Employment Act

- The Vietnam Era Veterans Readjustment Assistance Act

- The Rehabilitation Act of 1973

- The Equal Pay Act

- The National Labor Relations Act

- Executive Order 11242

- The Family and Medical Leave Act

This is just a sampling of the laws that determine what is appropriate and legal in the hiring process. In addition to federal law, each state has laws that also apply. To avoid problems involving legal liability, be sure to involve your corporate attorney in a regular review of your hiring practices and procedures.

TIP

> For complete information about state laws affecting the hiring process, Nolo.com has a Web site that allows you to search the statutes of each state. Their address is www.nolo.com/statutes/state.html.

DISPARATE TREATMENT AND DISPARATE IMPACT

"Disparate treatment" and "disparate impact" are the two basic legal concepts at the heart of Title VII of the Civil Rights Act of 1964, as well as similar civil rights legislation. It's important to understand what these terms mean to avoid the consequences that come with breaking the law, knowingly or in ignorance.

In a landmark 1977 case, the Supreme Court defined these two concepts in this manner:

> *Disparate treatment* ... is the most easily understood type of discrimination. The employer simply treats some people less favorably than others because of their race, color, religion, sex, or national origin. Proof of discriminatory motive is critical, although it can in some situations be inferred from the mere fact of differences in treatment.

> *Disparate impact* ... involves employment practices that are facially neutral in their treatment of different groups but that in fact fall more harshly on one group than another, and cannot be justified by business necessity .... Proof of discriminatory motive, we have held, is not required under disparate impact theory.

In layman's terms, here's what the court said:

> Disparate treatment occurs whenever a double standard is used in a selection process. Treating one candidate appreciably different than another is considered discriminatory. For example, asking women, but not men, whether their responsibilities at home might interfere with their employment is disparate treatment. So is asking someone whether church activities might keep that person from fulfilling the duties of the job for which they're applying.

Disparate impact takes place when one group of candidates is affected by a question more harshly than another. For example, asking whether candidates would mind working as part of an all-male workforce would have disparate impact on female applicants.

TIP

The best way to avoid becoming ensnared in nasty and expensive litigation is to make sure that every interview question you ask a candidate has a clear and direct business-related purpose.

INAPPROPRIATE QUESTIONS

A number of subject areas ought to be avoided in every job interview. These are the landmines that we talked about earlier. Some of them are always problematic; some can be rephrased in ways that make them legally palatable; some can be asked only after an offer of employment has been made.

Most of the subjects listed are not only inappropriate (or downright illegal) to include in interviews, but they also should not appear on your organization's formal employment application.

CAUTION

You could be held liable for obtaining potentially discriminatory information even if the applicant gives it voluntarily. If that occurs, it's best to change the subject immediately without making any notation whatsoever of the voluntary information.

MAIDEN NAME

Examples of inappropriate questions include these: "What was your maiden name?" "What was your father's surname?" "What was the last name you were born with?"

Asking an applicant to furnish a maiden name can be considered discriminatory in that it forces a female applicant to disclose her marital status.

Consider asking the candidate whether she is known by any other name by her former employers so that her work record can be obtained. This attaches a clear and direct business purpose to the question and makes it legal.

AGE

Examples of inappropriate questions include these: "What's your date of birth?"; "How old are you?"; "What year did you graduate from high school?"; "Are you near retirement age?"; "Aren't you too old to be applying for this kind of job?"; "Aren't you too young to be applying for a job that requires a good deal of experience?"

Asking an applicant to provide his or her date of birth, or asking how old that person is, focuses the interview on age rather than the qualifications of the applicant. Asking when an applicant graduated from high school enables the interviewer to calculate an approximate date of birth.

Although questions of this type are not expressly forbidden in Title VII, they could present formidable problems with candidates who are over 40 years of age and are thereby members of a protected class under the terms of the Age Discrimination in Employment Act.

If your purpose is to determine whether someone is of legal age for employment, ask if that person is 18 years of age or older. If you have any other purpose in asking the question, forget it. More than half the discrimination lawsuits filed in the United States each year are based on age discrimination. Don't become a statistic.

PLACE OF BIRTH/NATIONAL ORIGIN

Examples of inappropriate questions include these: "Where were you born?"; "What's your nationality?"; "What language do you speak in your home?"; "What languages do your parents speak?"; "Where did your family originally reside before coming to the United States?"; "How long have you lived at your present address?"

Title VII of the Civil Rights Act of 1964 prohibits discrimination in the workplace on the basis of national origin. In 1986, federal legislation known as the Immigration Reform and Control Act imposed the restrictions of the law on businesses with as few as four employees. Questions relating to one's place of birth invite claims of discrimination by unsuccessful applicants. So do questions regarding the birthplace of an applicant's family. Also taboo is asking an applicant to furnish a copy of a birth certificate or other papers demonstrating citizenship naturalization.

If your primary concern is whether a candidate has the legal right to hold a job in the United States, you could ask, "If you were hired, could you provide us with verification of your right to work in the United States?" If you need information as part of the federal *I-9* process, you may legally request the applicant for the information required for that purpose.

PLAIN ENGLISH

The I-9 Form   Section 274a of the Immigration and Nationality Act requires that employers verify that every employee hired after November 6, 1986, is authorized to work in the United States. This obligation applies to citizens and alien job applicants alike. Immigration and Naturalization Form I-9 outlines a formal process by which employers verify that candidates are legally able to work in the United States.

Also, employers may ask what languages a candidate speaks or writes fluently if there is a clear job-related purpose.

RELIGION

Examples of inappropriate questions include these: "What church do you attend?"; "We often require our employees to work weekends—would that be a problem for you?"; "What's the name of your pastor, priest, or rabbi?"; "Do you observe any special religious holidays?"

Title VII of the Civil Rights Act of 1964 prohibits any form of discrimination against employees or candidates for employment on the basis of religion. In fact, the Equal Employment Opportunity Commission states that Title VII "creates an obligation to provide *reasonable accommodation* for the religious practices of an employee or prospective employee unless to do so would create an undue hardship."

PLAIN ENGLISH

Reasonable accommodation   For religious practices, reasonable accommodation (without limitation) may include special work schedules designed to enable the employee to attend religious services or participate in religious observances. It may even include the possibility of transferring the employee to another job if that becomes necessary to accommodate the religious needs of the employee or candidate.

Several years ago, when I applied for a professional job in state government, I was told that I was "ruled out" as a viable candidate because I was an ordained Lutheran minister "who belonged in church work, not government." I didn't pursue the matter, but I could easily have done so.

It's frightening how many employers can't seem to understand that how employees (or potential employees) practice their religion is simply none of the employer's business unless the employer is asked to provide a reasonable accommodation. Not only does Title VII make that clear, but so does the First Amendment to the Constitution of the United States: "Congress shall make no law respecting an establishment of religion, or prohibiting the free exercise thereof."

If you make it a practice to discriminate on the basis of religion, you eventually will be sued—and you'll lose.

Periodically, I've read the work of some consultants who recommend making it a condition of employment when weekend work is mandatory. I suggest caution, however. Unless you've discussed the matter with your legal counsel, who is absolutely convinced that you can demonstrate that any other alternative would present an undue hardship on the organization, you're inviting litigation for discrimination.

I think it's preferable in situations in which weekend work is occasionally necessary for an employer to make it clear that a reasonable effort will be made to accommodate the religious needs of employees. This kind of language is certainly less offensive and is more in keeping with the spirit and letter of the law.

RACE OR COLOR

Issues of race and color normally do not arise as a result of questions posed in an interview. However, because unsuccessful candidates can raise claims of racial discrimination, I have included it here for your review.

Title VII of the Civil Rights Act of 1964 makes it unlawful for employers (or prospective employers) to discriminate on the basis of race, complexion, or color. There are no exceptions.

Those who feel that they have been discriminated against because of their race or color not only have the right to sue, but, under the provisions of The Civil Rights Act of 1991, they also have the right to a jury trial as well as the right to collect punitive and compensatory damages if the claim of discrimination is found to be valid.

Do not allow race or color to enter into the evaluation process. To the contrary, make it a practice to actively recruit minority applicants for positions within your organization. Make sure that you have a written plan to correct any areas of serious racial underrepresentation through an ongoing process of recruiting, hiring, training, and promoting minorities. (If your organization participates in federal contracts either as a primary contractor or a subcontractor, Executive Order 11242 mandates that such a plan be in effect.)

MARITAL STATUS

Examples of inappropriate questions include these: "Are you single or married?"; "Have you ever been married, divorced, separated, or widowed?"; "Do you prefer being called Ms., Mrs., or Miss?"; "What is your spouse's name?"; "Do you have any children?"; "Are you planning to have children within the next few years?"; "If you were to be employed, would locating suitable childcare be a problem?"

Title VII of the Civil Rights Act of 1964, along with a number of state antidiscrimination laws, make this area of employer inquiry a dangerous one. Unless there is a clear work-related reason for questions of this nature, it's best to avoid them altogether. Historically, questions about marital status have been used to discriminate against women.

Even when a candidate is obviously pregnant, it's best to avoid commenting on the fact in the pre-employment phase of the selection process. In 1978, Title VII was amended to include protection for women who are pregnant. Questions such as those indicated previously invite charges of sex discrimination by an unsuccessful job candidate.

Unless there is a clear job-related purpose, it's best to completely avoid questions of this nature. If a candidate mentions her pregnancy, it is advisable to simply change the subject. Do not make note of what she has told you concerning her pregnancy or her plans for subsequent childcare.

However, employers may inquire whether a candidate would be willing to relocate, if necessary. And, if travel is an essential function of the job, inquiries concerning the candidate's willingness to travel are appropriate as long as all candidates are asked the same questions.

HEALTH AND DISABILITY

Examples of inappropriate questions include these: "Are you disabled?"; "How many days of sick leave did you use last year?"; "Do you have any significant health problems?"; "Do you take prescription drugs regularly?"; "Have you ever filed a workman's compensation claim?"; "Do you have AIDS?"

The Americans with Disabilities Act of 1992 prohibits discrimination against qualified applicants whose disabilities would not prevent them from performing the essential functions of a job with or without a reasonable accommodation. This law applies to every business that employs 15 or more people, unless the business can demonstrate to the satisfaction of the Equal Employment Opportunity Commission that compliance with the law would present an undue hardship on the employer.

If you're concerned about whether a handicapped candidate can actually do the job, ask, "Are you capable of performing the essential functions of the job with or without an accommodation?"

After a conditional job offer has been made, an employer may require candidates to undergo a medical examination to determine their fitness for the job. Examination results can assist employers in determining specific accommodations that will enable the candidate to perform the essential functions of the job.

SEXUAL ORIENTATION

Examples of inappropriate questions include these: "Are you gay?"; "Are you lesbian?"; "Do you date other women (or men)?"

Although no specific federal laws prohibit employment discrimination on the basis of sexual orientation, several states offer legal protection for gays and lesbians. California, Massachusetts, Hawaii, Wisconsin, Vermont, Connecticut, New Jersey, and Minnesota have led the way.

Judge Sidney Asch of the New York State Supreme Court, Appellate Division, commenting on employment discrimination based on sexual orientation, said, "Where sexual proclivity does not relate to job function, it seems clearly unconstitutional to penalize an individual in one of the most imperative of life's endeavors, the right to earn one's daily bread."

It is only a matter of time before federal legislation makes this form of discrimination illegal. Unless you are prepared to demonstrate that being gay or lesbian adversely affects someone's ability to perform the essential functions of a job, don't inquire about sexual orientation.

ARRESTS

This is one example of an inappropriate question: "Have you ever been arrested?"

Although no specific federal laws prohibit inquiries about arrest records, several states have enacted legislation that would make this kind of question unlawful. Questions concerning a candidate's arrest record have been held to have an adverse discriminatory impact upon certain segments of the population. Under the disparate impact theory, questions about a candidate's arrest record could become the basis of a lawsuit for discrimination under Title VII of the Civil Rights Act of 1964.

While asking about the arrest record of a candidate for employment is risky business, employers may usually ask whether a candidate has ever been convicted of a crime. But be sure to check with your organization's attorney to determine whether the laws of your state may prohibit inquiries about an individual's conviction record, or whether state law limits the period of inquiry to a fixed number of months or years from the date of application.

CREDIT RECORDS

Examples of inappropriate questions include these: "Have you ever filed for bankruptcy?"; "Have you ever had your wages attached?"; "Are there any judgments against you?"

Such questions have been held to be unlawful when asked prior to a job offer being made. Employers may make an offer of employment contingent upon a credit check, as long as the employer abides by the conditions of all applicable state and federal laws, and can demonstrate that only those with good credit histories can perform the essential functions of the job.

Also, because some minority groups are economically disadvantaged, their credit histories tend to be adversely affected. Under the disparate impact theory, using credit information to make final employment decisions can be held discriminatory. Again, this is especially true when performance of the job is not affected by the poor credit history of the employee.

Be careful about using credit history. The burden of proof is clearly upon the employer to show a direct relationship between performance of the essential functions of a given job and the credit history of the employee. Be sure to consult your corporate attorney if you believe that credit checks are important to your selection process.

Union Membership

Examples of inappropriate questions include these: "Do you belong to a labor union?"; "Are you for or against labor unions?"; "Have you ever been a member of a labor union?"

The National Labor Relations Act prohibits the discrimination of employees or applicants for employment who are members of labor unions, or who favor membership in labor unions. Furthermore, the act prohibits employers from questioning employees or prospective employees about their union membership preference.

Avoid this kind of question altogether.

Military Service

Examples of inappropriate questions include these: "Have you ever served in the armed forces of another country?"; "If you've served in the U.S. military, did you receive an honorable discharge?"

Employers may ask about a candidate's U.S. military service but may not inquire about military service to another country. Questions about military service outside the United States may compel an applicant to disclose information about national origin, which may become the basis of a discrimination action.

When inquiring about a candidate's U.S. military service, frame your inquiries in such a way as to probe for skills and abilities acquired during the period that may have direct application to the job for which the applicant is being interviewed. The training that a candidate received as a member of the armed forces is usually valuable, and questions about it are always appropriate.

IN CASE OF EMERGENCY

Examples of inappropriate questions include these: "Please give us the name, address, and telephone number of your nearest relative whom we should notify in the event of an emergency."

Asking for the name of a *relative* could become the basis of a legal action for discrimination based on national origin, race, or even marital status.

The employer can't ask for a relative's name; limit this request to the name of "someone to contact in the event of an emergency." The candidate may provide the name of a relative in response to the question, of course.

CLUB MEMBERSHIPS

Examples of inappropriate questions include these: "What clubs do you participate in regularly?"; "List all the lodges, societies, and clubs to which you belong."

Unless you can demonstrate that this information is somehow related to the essential functions of the job, it's best to avoid this line of questioning completely. Club memberships may indicate the race, color, religion, national origin, or ancestry of its members; that information can become the basis of a discrimination action by an unsuccessful candidate.

Personal Information

Examples of inappropriate questions include these: "How tall are you?"; "How much do you weigh?"; "May we please have a photograph of you to attach to your application?"

Each of these questions is an example of an illegal pre-employment inquiry. Although this kind of information may have been routinely requested in applications for employment decades ago, today this is a surefire way to become embroiled in messy litigation.

Employers may inquire about the height and weight of a candidate if there are established minimum standards that have been determined to be essential for the safe performance of the job. In all other situations, personal questions of this nature should be avoided.

Hiring Without Being Sued

When managers don't ask the right questions (in interviews and in reference checks), their organizations run the risk of being sued for negligent hiring if the candidate is hired and later does something and someone gets hurt. Managers also run the risk of causing their organizations to be sued if they ask the wrong questions and learn things about a candidate that are unrelated to a candidate's qualifications and suitability for the job under discussion.

Managers must attend training seminars and workshops on hiring to help keep up-to-date with changes in employment and civil rights law. They should also work closely with their organizations' legal counsel whenever they have a question or concern about a hiring situation.

The 30-Second Recap

- Federal and state laws, as well as rulings from the courts, often regulate questions that can be legally asked of a candidate.

- Questions that are considered unlawful or inappropriate for interviews are similarly unlawful and inappropriate for use in employment applications.

- Interview questions should always be related to the essential functions of the job being sought.

- Avoiding potential legal problems involving claims of discrimination is the best strategy.

- Structured interviewing keeps the interview focused on job-related issues, thereby avoiding unplanned questions that can become the basis of discrimination claims.

LESSON 10
Active Listening Skills

In this lesson, you learn the importance of practicing good listening skills during the interview.

LISTENING ACTIVELY, TALKING FREELY

Several years ago, I completed a graduate program in therapeutic counseling. My hope was to be able to help people regain control of their lives after experiencing some type of psychological trauma.

One of the things I learned back then, and have since had reinforced more times than I care to count, is that counselors really can't help anyone until they know what the problem is—and counselors can't know what the problem is until clients tell them.

Active listening skills, one of the most important tools that a counselor has to work with, help encourage clients to talk freely and openly about problems and difficulties that they're facing. And the more freely a client talks about problems, the better equipped the counselor is to help. Getting people to talk about subjects that they may not want to discuss is the first step in any effective therapeutic intervention.

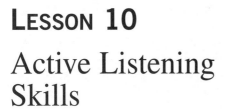

PLAIN ENGLISH

Active listening An interview technique, with origins in the field of psychotherapy, that helps assure candidates that the interviewer is listening to them intently. Active listening involves encouraging candidates to talk openly and freely by often reflecting back to them the meaning of their communication, both verbal and nonverbal, in ways that promote further exploration and awareness.

Interviewing candidates for employment involves the same basic challenge. To hire the right person for a job, it's necessary to gain a real understanding of each candidate who applies. It's important to know who they are, how they think, what their goals and aspirations are, and whether they have the competencies needed to be successful in the job.

But to evaluate each candidate fairly and accurately, the interviewer must obtain the necessary information, and that means getting the candidate to talk even about subjects that may be uncomfortable to discuss (past failures, weaknesses, problems with former employers or co-workers, and so on). The more the candidate talks, the better the interviewer understands the candidate and can decide whether he or she is qualified for the position.

 TIP

> Be sure that your questions about a candidate's weaknesses or past failures have direct application to the job he or she is seeking. Past problems that involve a candidate's personal life are not appropriate for discussion during the interview process.

The Benefits of Active Listening

Active listening skills promote warmth and honest communication. But even more important, they help strip away superficial levels of *communication* by encouraging candidates to talk about skill-related experiences and the deeper personal meanings that often accompany them.

 PLAIN ENGLISH

> **Communication**   Any means (verbal or nonverbal) of giving information or news to another. One of the main functions of communication in the context of a job interview is to impart knowledge, and provide job-related information.

Here are some of the benefits of active listening, along with some typical interviewer responses that help bring them about:

- Active listening demonstrates to a candidate that the interviewer is intensely interested in what's being said: "You seem to be saying that you have felt undervalued in your present employment and that you feel frustrated as a result."

- Even more important, it demonstrates that the candidate has not only been heard, but also understood: "If I'm hearing you correctly, you would like a chance to work for a company that would value someone with your skills and abilities."

- It provides an opportunity for the interviewer to discover and correct any misunderstandings or inaccurate interpretations that may develop during the course of an interview: "If I understand you correctly, you like the company you're presently working for, but you dislike your immediate supervisor. Is that correct?"

- It communicates unconditional acceptance to the candidate, which encourages further exploration: "You feel undervalued in your present work."

- It keeps the focus where it belongs—on the candidate and the specific behavior being probed: "It seems that you feel that your ability to lead others is being overlooked in your present employment, and that you want to find employment that will allow you to not only manage, but also lead. Is that correct?"

- It encourages deeper levels of communication: "You want to be recognized for your leadership abilities …. Tell me about a time when you were placed in a leadership role. What is there about it that you liked? What did you dislike?"

- It encourages open and honest communication: "You say that you resent not having a leadership role in your present job, and you seem hurt by it."

How to Listen Actively

Active listening, as the term implies, requires active participation on the part of the listener; the listener does more than just listen. It calls for the listener to become actively involved in the process of communication by periodically confirming understanding of what's being said by the speaker. Developing active listening skills demands practice.

When using active listening while conducting job interviews, there are several important points to remember.

First, be genuinely curious about what the applicant is saying. Even if you're tempted to tune out because you've heard the question and the usual response a hundred times, force yourself to be curious about what the candidate is saying.

TIP

Make an effort to engage with the candidate, and suddenly you'll find yourself taking real interest in what's being said. There's nothing more encouraging to a candidate than to have an interviewer really listen and to confirm that listening with appropriate questions or statements.

Second, don't be judgmental. When a candidate makes statements that you disagree with, don't voice your disagreement. Remember that this is the candidate's opportunity to tell a story about the use of a certain skill or ability, or simply to express an opinion. Reserve your judgment for the evaluation phase of the process—that's where it belongs. During the interview, focus only on making sure that you understand exactly what the candidate is saying.

Third, make a conscious effort to resist distractions, whether internal or external. Active listening requires total concentration on what's being said. Control those distractions that are controllable so that the concentration of everyone participating in the interview process remains unbroken.

Fourth, reflect content back to the candidate. When you tell candidates what you think they're saying, you encourage them to continue speaking, you show sincere interest in their presentations, and you demonstrate concern for the accuracy of the message they're conveying.

Fifth, listen for the emotions behind a candidate's words. Those emotions can include happiness, sadness, fear, disappointment, frustration, anxiety, and every other emotion. When you hear a candidate talking in emotional terms, learn more about why the emotional response is there by saying, "You sound frustrated with your present job. What is there about it that frustrates you most?"

Sixth, don't interrupt a candidate with a follow-up question. Sometimes while you're actively listening to a candidate, you'll suddenly think of an important follow-up question that simply must be asked. When that happens, jot it down and ask it later. Interrupting a candidate who's attempting to answer specific behavioral questions is a little like throwing cold water on a fire.

And seventh, while we're on the subject of note taking, plan to take plenty of notes about what the candidate says. Not only does note taking demonstrate the importance of what's being said, but it also will prove invaluable when it comes time to evaluate candidates.

FACILITATIVE AND INHIBITING INTERVIEWER RESPONSES

The manner in which the interviewer responds to a candidate will either facilitate communication or inhibit it. The following is a list of *facilitative responses* that will help you listen actively:

- Unconditional acceptance ("That must have been very difficult for you. Thank you for sharing your feelings with us.")

- Obvious open-mindedness ("That's an interesting way of looking at that situation.")

- Open behavioral questions.

- Patience ("Take your time.")

- Reflective comments.

- Positive reinforcement.

- Empathetic remarks.

- Support comments.

- Structuring.

- Supportive body language.

Inhibiting responses will keep a candidate from speaking freely and deeply about important matters. Here are a few of the most common inhibiting responses:

- Criticism.

- Rejection.

- Moralistic responses ("I never would have believed that anyone would actually do something like that.")

- Self-indulgent disclosures ("Sometimes people ask me about the secret to my financial success in life and I tell them that since I was a lad I've always saved 10 percent of everything I earn, and I give another 10 percent to charity. I've always felt that if you can't live on 80 percent of your income, you can't live on 100 percent of it either.")

- Belittling statements.

- Intolerance.

- Dogmatic statements.

- Sarcasm.

- Obvious impatience.

- Allowed Distractions.

PLAIN ENGLISH

Facilitative responses   The responses of an interviewer that encourage a candidate to talk freely about the areas explored in the interview. **Inhibiting responses**   Those responses of an interviewer that prevent candidates from wanting to talk about important matters. Facilitative responses produce excellent interviews; inhibiting responses are destructive.

Nonverbal Cues

Body language has become a hot topic in human resources circles over the past few years. Body language can be revealing, but sometimes an interviewer can get the wrong message entirely.

For example, some people routinely hold their chin in their palm hand when they're contemplating something important. But in an interview session, this kind of body language could easily be interpreted as suggesting someone who is unfocused and inattentive.

Over the years, I've developed the habit of sitting with my arms crossed while carrying on a business-related conversation. But in an interview situation, that kind of body language could be interpreted as evidence of closed-mindedness and defensive posturing.

TIP

Make an effort to examine your own unique body language, especially during interview sessions. Try to avoid body language that may conflict with the principles of active listening.

The Candidate's Nonverbal Cues

When you encounter a candidate whose body language seems to communicate one thing but whose verbal responses seem to communicate something else, it's usually best to check your interpretations of these nonverbal cues with the candidate. Do so in a way that doesn't cause embarrassment, but be direct. Ask the candidate if your interpretation of a certain body language is correct. ("It seems that whenever we discuss your present employment your body language appears to indicate a reluctance to discuss the matter in any detail. Is there a reason for that? Or, am I simply misinterpreting your body language?")

Also, remember that you have no idea of the context of the interview in the life of the candidate. A number of years ago, I interviewed a young lady for a professional position for which she seemed eminently qualified. During the interview, however, she became distracted and unfocused. Her body language suggested extreme anxiety.

I attempted to confirm the message from her body language by asking whether she was feeling anxious about the interview. The young lady began to sob uncontrollably. When I inquired what was wrong, she said that a few hours beforehand, she had received a telephone call from her sister telling her of her father's sudden death. In spite of the news, she attempted to muster up enough strength to complete the interview, but the news proved too overwhelming.

Had I relied only on the nonverbal cues presented by the candidate, I would have probably concluded that the job and the candidate were not a good match. But having inquired further, I learned that it was the context of the interview that was the problem, not the candidate. We rescheduled our interview for another time, and the young lady was eventually hired and today manages an entire division of the same firm.

Always confirm nonverbal cues with a candidate. Body language can be prompted by many things other than the interview—or, for that matter, nothing at all.

The Interviewer's Nonverbal Cues

From the standpoint of active listening, what's really important is the interviewer's nonverbal cues. To communicate acceptance, interest, and support, the interviewer should practice making eye contact with the candidate while leaning slightly forward from a seated position.

Eye contact should be broken only when notes are being written or other members of the interview panel are being addressed.

Be careful not to convey boredom by paying attention to something other than what the candidate is saying, by yawning, or by constantly looking at your watch or a room clock. These kinds of messages can put a real damper on what might otherwise be a good interview.

When the interviewer mentally engages with the candidate and practices good active listening skills, nonverbal communication usually takes care of itself.

THE 30-SECOND RECAP

- Active listening is a technique that has its roots in psychotherapy and helps encourage candidates to talk freely and openly about behavioral situations.

- Active listening helps move an interview from superficial levels to deeper levels, giving the interviewer an opportunity to gain a better understanding of the person being interviewed.

- Among other important benefits, active listening provides the interviewer an opportunity to immediately clear up any misunderstandings or to obtain needed clarification.

- Interviewers should be constantly aware of the messages that they are giving applicants through verbal and nonverbal forms of communication. How an interviewer responds to a candidate (verbally and nonverbally) will be either facilitative or inhibiting.

LESSON 11

Conducting the Interview

In this lesson, you follow a general sales manager for XYZ Corporation step by step as he constructs a sample structured behavioral interview.

So far, you've learned to begin the interview process with an analysis of the job to determine the mandatory success factors; you've learned how to review resumés and to prescreen candidates to interview; you've learned about the process of structured behavioral interviewing; and you've learned how to develop behavioral questions that seek out essential competencies.

Now it's time to put it all to work to construct an actual interview.

THE MODEL

XYZ Corporation is about to lose an important member of its team. For the past 15 years, John Jones has occupied the position of district sales manager for one of the company's most profitable geographic regions. John is scheduled to retire in two months, and recruitment activities to find a suitable replacement are about to begin.

Pete Smith, the general sales manager for the company, provides direct supervision of each of the company's district sales managers, so he will take the lead in recruiting and evaluating candidates. Although the final hiring decision will be made by him, Pete decides to enlist the help of one salesman, one district sales manager, and one home office support supervisor to assist him in the selection process.

JOB ANALYSIS

Pete begins by taking a hard look at the job being vacated. He reviews the formal position description and talks at length with John to learn John's perspective on what it takes to succeed as a district sales manager, and to learn about any unique requirements that may exist in his particular district. He talks with members of John's sales team to obtain their input on what's needed in a new sales manager. He talks with other home office managers and support staff who regularly work with district sales managers to get their advice on what to look for in a new sales manager.

As a result of his investigation, and based on his own knowledge of the job, Pete has developed the following position profile.

TECHNICAL COMPETENCIES

The following company-mandated competencies are required of all district sales managers:

- A bachelor's degree in business administration, sales administration, marketing, or a closely allied field
- A minimum of five years of successful experience managing a sales organization

FUNCTIONAL SKILLS

From his own observations, and from talking with others, Pete makes a list of the functional skills that the new district sales manager should possess:

- Communication skills (oral and written)
- Management skills
- Training and mentoring
- Leadership
- Independence

- Teamwork
- Initiative
- Customer service
- Sales ability
- Public relations ability
- Development of subordinates
- Detail orientation
- Listening ability
- Supervision ability
- Planning and organizing ability

SELF-MANAGEMENT SKILLS

In addition, here are some suggested personal characteristics that would help a district sales manager to succeed with the company:

- Ethics
- Honesty
- Loyalty
- Reliability
- Accountability
- Self-sufficiency

INTERPERSONAL SKILLS

For the position of district sales manager, good interpersonal skills are important to the successful performance of the job, especially the ability to do the following:

- Empathize and care about the concerns of others.
- Listen actively and attentively.

- Remain objective without becoming emotional.

- Communicate effectively with others.

THE CORPORATE CULTURE

XYZ Corporation prides itself in the professionalism of its employees. Although it's an unwritten mandate, the company really wants each of its key employees (district sales managers among them) to adhere to the following:

- Constantly be involved in some form of formal training that will contribute to their ability to perform quality work in a professional manner.

- Attend all sales conferences and seminars sponsored by the company.

- Actively participate in state and national associations in which the company holds membership.

DETERMINING MANDATORY SUCCESS FACTORS

Having identified the competencies, skills, and abilities that the ideal candidate would possess, it's time for Pete to narrow the field to those factors that are absolutely necessary for success on the job. With this in mind, Pete proceeds to rate each skill in order of its importance to job success, identifying the top five functional skills and the top two self-management skills from the other skills listed.

TIP

Rating skills in order of their importance to the successful performance of a job is also something that can be done by the entire selection team. This procedure may be a bit more time consuming, but the extra input is well worth it.

Here are the results:

Functional skills:

1. Teamwork (Weighted by 5)

2. Training and mentoring (Weighted by 4)

3. Communication skills (Weighted by 3)

4. Leadership (Weighted by 2)

5. Customer service (Weighted by 1)

TIP

For purposes of weighting each of the factors in the evaluation process, take the number of factors being considered (in this case, five), and assign that number to the most important factor. Weighting for functional skills indicated here would be: teamwork (5), training (4), communication (3), leadership (2), and customer service (1) (see Appendix B, "Interview Evaluation Summary").

PLAIN ENGLISH

Weight factor   A number that is assigned to each mandatory success factor being evaluated. The score for each mandatory success factor is multiplied by the weight factor to determine the total number of points awarded.

Self-management skills:

1. Honesty

2. Reliability

TIP

You can identify as many skills in each category as you want. However, from a practical standpoint, it's best to identify a limited number of skills in each category.

The skills identified in this process are the mandatory success factors for the position of district sales manager. These are the factors that will guide Pete as he develops structured behavioral questions and associated follow-up probes; these are also the objective factors upon which he and his team will evaluate candidates.

Notice that technical competencies, interpersonal skills, and requirements of the corporate culture were not prioritized. That's because each of these requirements is already considered mandatory.

A review of the candidate's application and resumé will help determine whether the candidate possesses the required technical competencies. Specific questions concerning interpersonal skills (if not already covered in the functional skill area) will need to be developed, as will questions concerning the candidate's ability to assimilate successfully into the corporate culture.

CONSTRUCTING BEHAVIORAL QUESTIONS

Now that the mandatory success factors have been identified, it's time to begin constructing behavioral questions that will elicit real-life evidence of a candidate's level of competence with each factor.

TEAMWORK

This is the most important success factor identified. Teamwork involves working well with others for the purpose of accomplishing organizational goals, or to identify and solve problems.

Behavioral question: "Tell me about a time when you used a team approach to problem solving."

Follow-up probes:

- "How did the team work?"

- "What solutions did you attempt before involving the team?"

- "What were your responsibilities on the team?"

- "What specific actions did the team take?"

- "What obstacles needed to be overcome by the team in solving the problem?"

- "What results did the team achieve?"

Notice that each of the follow-up questions is designed to guide the candidate's response. Remember the STAR formula: Behavioral responses should discuss a specific situation or task, provide detailed information concerning actions taken by the candidate, and conclude with a discussion of the result achieved.

TRAINING AND MENTORING

District sales managers for XYZ Company are responsible for training and mentoring new sales staff, as well as continually developing existing staff. This function involves formal training sessions at the district office. It also involves regularly working with each member of the sales team in field situations, providing one-to-one coaching and skill-building activities.

Behavioral question: "Describe a time when you hired a new salesperson who knew very little about how to succeed in selling your company's product. What kind of help did you provide?"

Follow-up probes:

- "What kinds of training techniques do you think work particularly well?"

- "What kinds of one-to-one activities have you participated in with new salespeople to help them achieve success?"

- "Tell us about a time when a salesperson refused to see things your way. What did you do?"

- "What is a mentor? Give us an example of a time when you mentored someone."

- "Tell us about the impact that your training and mentoring activities have had on your past success as a sales manager."

COMMUNICATION SKILLS

The job of the district sales manager for XYZ Company requires the ability to express ideas orally and in writing. Over the years, many of those who have failed in this job lacked the ability to communicate effectively.

Behavioral question: "Describe a situation in which you made an oral presentation of a written proposal that you prepared."

Follow-up probes:

- "What were the most important elements of the proposal?"

- "What are some things that you did to strengthen the presentation?"

- "What could you have done to make the presentation better?"

- "What kinds of things have you done since that time to enhance your communication skills? What do you intend to do in the near future?"

- "Tell us about the outcome of your proposal."

LEADERSHIP

The district sales manager must be a leader and must lead by example. At XYZ Company, sales managers succeed only when they are able to lead others to success.

Behavioral question: "If I were to call your present supervisor, how would she describe your leadership ability?" (For this factor, Pete decides to use a self-appraisal question.)

Follow-up probes:

- "Tell me about a time when your ability to lead really paid off."

- "What kinds of things do you do that mark you as a strong leader?"

- "What results have you achieved through your leadership abilities?"

CUSTOMER SERVICES

At XYZ Company, customer satisfaction is a high priority. Listening to the needs of customers, understanding them, and responding in an appropriate and timely manner is essential.

Behavioral question: "Tell us about the most difficult customer service experience you've ever had to handle."

Follow-up probes:

- "How were you made aware of the problem?"

- "What steps did you take to solve the situation?"

- "What could you have done better?"

- "What happened as a result of your intervention?"

BEHAVIORAL PROBES FOR SELF-MANAGEMENT SKILLS

Developing behavioral questions for self-management skills is accomplished in much the same way as it is for functional skills. However, follow-up probes are often noticeably different.

Because the self-management skill set usually involves strongly held beliefs and attitudes, follow-up probes tend to be more exploratory in nature. The STAR response is not always what's needed to properly assess this type of factor. This is especially true when questions are phrased as continuum or self-appraisal questions.

HONESTY

XYZ Company believes that honesty is the cornerstone of its business. The company prides itself in dealing honestly and fairly with its customers as well as its employees, and expects the same kind of treatment in return.

Behavioral question: "On a scale between being absolutely honest and absolutely committed to making things work at any cost, where do you fit?" (For this factor, Pete decides to use a continuum question.)

Follow-up probes:

- "Tell me about a time when you bent the truth a bit to accomplish an important goal."

- "Describe a situation in which telling the truth lost you the sale or caused you to lose in some other way."

- "Give us an example of a time when you discovered some dishonesty in someone reporting to you. What did you do?"

RELIABILITY

"A man's word is his bond." That's hardly a twenty-first century idea, and many might even consider it old-fashioned and antiquated. But at XYZ Corporation, it's more than a motto; it's a performance expectation.

Behavioral question: "Give us an example of a time when keeping your word to a customer or an employee meant having to endure a good deal of personal difficulty."

Follow-up probes:

- "What was so important about the commitment?"

- "What was required of you to keep your promise?"

- "What happened as a result of your efforts to keep your word?"

- "Tell me about someone you know who is absolutely reliable."

- "Are you always reliable?"

THE INTERVIEW PLAN

Now that the behavioral questions and follow-up probes for each mandatory success factor have been developed, the next step is to plan the interview process itself. Here's a step-by-step interview model that I've used several times and can highly recommend.

TIP

> Be sure to make any modifications necessary to customize the interview plan for use in your organization. Also, times indicated are merely suggested and should be altered to fit the needs of a specific interview.

Introductory phase: 5–10 minutes

- Introduce the candidate to each member of the interview team and ask panel members to introduce themselves.

- Inform the candidate of how the interview will be conducted (who will be asking primary questions, follow-up questions, and so on.)

- Inform the candidate of when you expect the interview to be concluded.

- Ask any questions necessary to clear up questions concerning the candidate's application or resumé.

Information-gathering phase: 1 hour

- Ask primary behavioral questions. (5 percent)
- Probe for specific actions. (65 percent)
- Probe for additional information or clarification. (20 percent)
- Probe for results. (10 percent)

Repeat this process until each of your mandatory success factors has been probed.

Position description phase: 5 minutes

- Provide the candidate with a job description.
- Explain the duties and responsibilities of the position.
- Offer specific examples of work performed.
- Offer to answer questions concerning the position.

Sell the company: 5 minutes

Be sure to assign one member of the interview team the responsibility of "selling the company" to the candidate. This should be a true sales effort outlining the major benefits involved in working for the company.

The Closing Phase: 5–10 minutes

- Ask if the candidate has any unanswered questions.
- Ask if the candidate is interested in pursuing the position.
- Inform the candidate of what the next step will be in the selection process and when a decision is likely to be made.

THE 30-SECOND RECAP

- Begin with an analysis of the job—be sure to solicit the input of others.

- Identify required technical competencies, "ideal candidate" functional skills, "ideal candidate" self-management skills, interpersonal skill requirements, and any special requirements of the corporate culture.

- Rate the "ideal candidate" functional and self-management skills to determine which of them are mandatory success factors.

- Develop behavioral interview questions and follow-up probes for each of the mandatory success factors, the interpersonal skill requirements, and the requirements of the corporate culture.

- Develop an interview plan that will provide an agenda for the interview process and define general time allotments.

LESSON 12
Critique and Fine Tune

In this lesson, you learn the value of constructively critiquing the interviews that you conduct to spot weaknesses and other difficulties that may need to be corrected.

INTERVIEW CHECKLIST

The price of building and maintaining good interviewing skills and techniques is eternal vigilance. After each round of interviews, it helps to take a few minutes to critique the interview process to detect what went right and what may need improvement.

Here's a checklist covering each of the major tasks involved in the interview process. Use it to help spot weak areas and to reinforce strengths.

PREINTERVIEW

- A thorough analysis of the vacant position was performed, and mandatory success factors were identified.

- The immediate supervisor of the position was asked to describe any special factors that may be required to succeed in the job, including those imposed by the corporate culture.

- An interview panel was assembled, consisting of all supervisors to whom the new employee will report, together with a peer or two from the department or unit in which the opening exists.

- Panel members met at least once to thoroughly discuss the interview process.

- A resumé review tool, such as the Resumé Review Grid, discussed in Lesson 2, "The Resumé," was developed and used as part of the preinterview screening process.

- Resumés were screened by more than one person.

- Applicants eliminated in the initial screening process were notified in writing.

TIP

> Remember that just because an applicant was eliminated from further consideration for one job doesn't mean you'll never be interested in hiring them. The next opening in your organization may be a perfect match. So take the time to contact each unsuccessful applicant, thanking them for their interest, and encouraging them to apply again (unless, of course, the reason for their elimination is something that will disqualify them from being employed in any capacity with your firm.)

- Specific concerns about information contained in resumés (See the section "Red Flags," in Lesson 2) were clearly flagged for further discussion with the candidate.

- All candidates selected for further consideration were notified in writing and were asked to complete company employment application forms, which included a clause permitting you to contact any and all former employers as well as others with knowledge of the applicant's work history, and a hold harmless agreement permitting all references to release information about the applicant.

TIP

> Be sure to ask your corporate attorney to periodically review your company's employment application to ensure that you have the proper legal authority to "network" references—that is, to ask each of them to provide a name of someone else who is familiar with the applicant's work.

- Candidates were also asked to submit 10 "personal" references that included the names of former employers.

- Behavioral questions and appropriate follow-up probes were developed for each of the mandatory success factors identified in the job review.

- Any required testing was arranged for each candidate selected to be interviewed.

- References were contacted prior to interviews.

- Academic degrees were verified prior to interviews.

- Interviews were scheduled in advance, and sufficient time was allocated for each interview.

INTERVIEW

- Interviews were held in an area that was free from noise and interruption.

- Panel members were briefed about the candidate before each interview and were given a copy of the candidate's resumé, together with the comments of reviewers who initially reviewed it.

- Panel members were punctual and prepared for the interview process.

- An attempt was made to put candidates at ease before each interview.

- In the opening segment of the interview, candidates were told what to expect during the interview.

- Candidates were asked to explain any questions raised in the initial review of their resumé.

- The 80/20 rule was followed—the candidate did at least 80 percent of the talking.

- Each member of the interview panel practiced active listening skills during the interviews.

- Panel members maintained eye contact with each candidate.

- The behavioral questions developed for each mandatory success factor were asked of all candidates interviewed.

- Candidates were allowed sufficient time to answer questions.

- Candidates were given verbal and nonverbal encouragement during the course of interviews.

- The course of each interview was appropriately controlled.

- Interviews were focused on mandatory success factors and didn't drift into areas not related to the position being sought.

- Interview panel members took appropriate notes during the course of each interview.

- At the end of each interview, candidates were told what comes next.

- Candidates were given a positive impression of the company because one member of the interview panel took responsibility for "selling the company" to each candidate.

- During the closing segment of the interview process, candidates were given an opportunity to ask questions about the job and the company.

Postinterview

- Evaluations of candidates were completed immediately following each interview, using an appropriate evaluation tool (see Lesson 6, "Structured Behavioral Interviewing: Part 1.")

- The candidate of choice was hired, with the decision being promptly communicated to all remaining candidates, or a short list of top candidates was developed.

- Second interviews were scheduled for short-listed candidates utilizing alternative interview methods.

- Feedback from those involved in second interview situations was evaluated.

- The candidate of choice was hired, with the decision being promptly communicated to all remaining candidates.

Make It a Habit

Each part of the interview process is important. Whether you're new to structured behavioral interviewing or have been doing it for years, there's always room for improvement.

Make it a habit to regularly review the interview process and to make improvements whenever necessary. Continue to look for ways to develop your style of interviewing.

The 30-Second Recap

- Critiquing interviews helps the manager to fine tune the interview process for maximum effectiveness.

- Regardless of your personal experience with structured behavioral interview techniques, there's always room for improvement.

- Checklists, similar to the one outlined in this lesson, are a good way to objectively review the interview process.

- Remember that the objective is to find the best candidate for the job. So, retain and improve whatever process steps help accomplish that goal, and improve or eliminate whatever gets in the way of it.

APPENDIX A

Sample Interview Questions

Here are some sample behavioral questions, along with a few suggested follow-up probes, that you can use in future interviews. Feel free to adapt them to fit your unique situation. You'll also want to expand the number of follow-up probes that you use.

Because these questions are behavioral in nature, there are no right or wrong answers. They're meant to help you discover behavioral evidence of a candidate's ability to successfully perform the job in question.

Remember to use the STAR formula (see Lesson 7, "Structured Behavioral Interviewing: Part 2") to gather the information that you'll need to make an accurate evaluation of the candidate's skills and abilities (**s**ituation or **t**ask, **a**ctions taken, **r**esults).

ACCOUNTABILITY

- Tell me about a time when a project or task under your direction didn't measure up to expectations. What happened? Who was at fault?

- Give me an example of a time when you were accountable for the subpar work of others. How did you respond to the situation with your superiors? In what ways did you hold those working for you accountable?

ADAPTABILITY

- Describe a time when you had to adapt to a wide variety of people, situations, and environments. How difficult is it for you to adapt to new situations? What techniques have you discovered to be helpful?

- (Continuum) On a scale between liking constant sameness and liking constant change, where do you fit? Tell me about a job you've had in the past that involved a good deal of change.

ANALYTICAL SKILLS

- Relate a story in which you were given a work assignment that involved lots of analysis. What did you do to gather the needed information? What kinds of help did you need to complete the assignment?

- (Self-appraisal) If I were to ask your present supervisor about your analytical skills, what would she tell me? What does it take to perform good analysis? How did you develop your analytical skills?

ASSERTIVENESS

- We've all been involved in situations in which we've had to speak up to get our point across. Tell me about a time when you had to be assertive. What was at stake? What risks did you take in being assertive? How difficult is it for you to become assertive in a situation?

- Describe a time when you felt that something at work was happening that was unfair to yourself or others. What did you do? How did others perceive your action? What did you accomplish?

CLOSING TECHNIQUES

- Describe a time when you were working with a difficult customer but ended up closing the sale. What did you do to make it happen? What closing techniques do you use effectively? How many times should one attempt to close a sale before giving up altogether?

- Describe the most difficult sale you've ever made. Why were you successful? What's the most common objection you face in sales? How do you overcome it? How do you handle objections based on misunderstanding?

COMMUNICATION SKILLS

- Tell me about a time when you were asked to make a presentation on a business-related topic. What was the topic? How did you prepare? What things did you do to make your presentation interesting and effective? Did you use visual aids? Are you familiar with Microsoft PowerPoint?

- Relate a story about a work situation in which your communication skills were really put to the test. How important of a role have communication skills had in the development of your career? What types of communication do you feel you are particularly good at?

CONFLICT MANAGEMENT

- Recall for me a time when you had a disagreement with your boss. What prompted the disagreement? What did you do to convince your boss that your position was the correct one? How was the situation resolved?

- Tell me of a time when you had a conflict with a co-worker. What was involved? How did you handle it? Was compromise a part of your solution?

CONFRONTATION

- Give me an example of a recent confrontation that you had with an employee whose results were unacceptable. What did you do to prepare for the confrontation? Where was the physical location of the confrontation? What was your objective in confronting the employee and was it achieved?

- Tell me about the last time that a superior confronted you with a problem. What was involved? How did you handle the situation? How was the matter resolved?

CREATIVITY

- Describe a time in which you were allowed to be completely creative in your work. How did it feel? What about the project did you find energizing? Give me a few examples of creative projects that you've been involved with in the past.

- Tell me about the most significant creative presentation you've made. What was there about the presentation that worked? What could you have done better?

CUSTOMER SERVICE SKILLS

- Tell me about the most difficult customer you've ever encountered. What did you do to satisfy the customer? Was it enough? What could you have done better? What do you think is the most important principle governing customer service? What kinds of things do you do to ensure that this principle is always followed?

- Describe a situation in which you dealt with a customer who insisted that he was right when you knew that he was wrong. Were you successful? What did it take? What is your philosophy of customer service? Considering your present employer's customer service policies, tell us about the ones that work well.

DECISION MAKING

- Tell me about a situation in which you were forced to make a decision about something not covered by company policy. How did you go about making the decision? How did you involve others in the process?

- Describe the most difficult business decision you've ever made. What was at stake? Who was involved? What resources did you use in making the decision?

Delegating

- Give me an example of a time when you were assigned a major project. How did you select those who would participate with you? How did you manage those to whom project assignments were given?

- Tell me about a time when you delegated work to someone who didn't complete it in an acceptable manner. How did you handle the matter?

Dependability

- Give me an example of a time when you had to go above and beyond the call of duty to get the job done. What was at stake? What was the payoff? Where did the extra energy come from?

- Tell me about a time when you had to sacrifice personal plans to complete a job-related task. Was anyone other than you affected by your sacrifice? If so, how would that person rate your dependability?

Detail Orientation

- Tell me about a time when you were in charge of a major project involving a multiplicity of detail. How did you manage the project while paying attention to each detail? How important to the outcome are the details of a project?

- The last time you were assigned a major project, how did you go about planning the work to be done? What tools did you use? What methods did you rely upon to ensure quality work completed in a timely manner?

DISCIPLINE

- Tell me about the last time you disciplined an employee. What was involved? How did you proceed? What was your objective? What success did you achieve?

- Considering the last time you had to terminate an employee, what could have been done to prevent the termination? What could the company have done better? What could you have done better?

EDUCATION

- Of all your past educational experiences (formal and informal), which ones were most helpful in qualifying you for this job? What kinds of skills did you acquire as a result of that training?

- Describe a time when your education made a significant difference in your accomplishments on the job. Be specific.

EMPATHY

- Relate a story about a time when your ability to empathize with an employee or customer really paid off. How well can you know what someone else is feeling? What's the difference between empathy and sympathy?

- (Continuum) On a continuum between being empathetic to others and being dogmatic about policy and procedure, where would you fit?

ENJOYMENT

- Recall for me a job or a project that you particularly enjoyed. What was there about it that you found enjoyable? What do you enjoy about your present job?

- Tell me about the businessperson you most admire. What is it that this person enjoys about his or her job? If you could create your dream job, what elements would you include that would give you enjoyment?

ENTHUSIASM

- Tell me of a time when you needed to motivate others. How did you do it? What is the best way you've found to motivate others?

- Relate a personal story about a time when you simply couldn't become enthusiastic about a project or a task. Did you proceed in spite of your lack of enthusiasm? Was the work completed successfully? How did your lack of enthusiasm affect others?

ETHICS

- Tell me about a time when your personal ethics would not permit you to obey the direction of a superior. How did you handle the situation? What were the risks? What was the result?

- (Contrary evidence) What things do you consider unethical? Tell me about a time when you've become aware that someone you knew acted unethically in one of the ways you just described.

EXPERIENCE

- Tell me about the experiences you've had with your present employer that you feel are most valuable to you. What have you learned? How would you propose to share the same experiences with those who will work for you?

- Describe how your previous work experiences qualify you for the job you're seeking. Be specific.

FACT FINDING

- Describe a project that involved a good deal of fact finding. How did you approach the task? In what ways did the fact-finding mission contribute to the success of the project?

- Describe a time when you gathered facts from many different sources to create something important. What forms of research did you use to discover the facts that you needed? How did you organize your search? What did the final product look like?

FAIRNESS

- Give me an example of a situation that involved absolute fairness in dealing with a problem employee. What was involved in treating the employee fairly? What extraordinary things did your commitment to fairness cause you to do? What did fairness achieve?

- Relate a personal story about how you were treated unfairly by a former employer. When did it occur? What was involved? How did that treatment affect your attitude toward that employer?

FLEXIBILITY

- Describe a situation in which extreme flexibility was important to the successful performance of your job. How important do you think it is to be flexible in the job you're seeking? Why? What's the downside to being extremely flexible?

- Tell me about a situation in which your lack of flexibility hurt your overall job performance. How did you correct the situation? Tell me about a situation in which being flexible was difficult for you in some way.

FOLLOWING DIRECTIONS

- (Continuum) On a scale between working creatively and following the directions of others, where do you fit?

- Tell me about a time when you disagreed with something that you were told to do, but did it anyway. To whom did you voice your disagreement? What was that person's response? Would you have handled the matter any differently had you been in charge?

FORESIGHTEDNESS

- Give me an example of a time when you averted a major problem by using foresight. What does foresight on the job involve?

- Tell me about a time when a failure at work could have been avoided had you only used a little foresight. What did you learn from the experience?

FRUSTRATION

- Describe the most frustrating aspect of your present job. What could be done to make your job less frustrating? Have you suggested changes? What do you do to cope with the frustrating aspects of your present job?

- Tell me about a time when someone at work was frustrated by something you did. How did you find out about the frustration? Could you do anything to correct the situation? If so, what did you do? If not, what would you do differently?

HELP

- What did you do in your last job to help new employees get started on the right track? Did your efforts accomplish your objective?

- Tell me about a time when you needed the help of a more experienced manager to help you accomplish an important mission. How did you know whom to ask for help? When was the last time another manager asked for your help?

HIRING

- Tell me the biggest hiring mistake you've made as a manager. When were you first aware that a hiring mistake was probably made? In hindsight, were there any indications in the interview process that there may be problems with this particular candidate? If you had it to do all over again, are there areas that you would have probed more intensely in the interview process?

- Tell me about your use of structured behavioral interviewing. What do you see as the strengths of this method over conventional models? Are employees who have been selected using this interview method more likely to be successful on the job? Why, or why not?

HONESTY

- Relate a situation in which your sense of personal honesty defined the manner in which you accomplished a particular task. Is absolute honesty in business affairs possible?

- Tell me about a time when it appeared that someone's dishonesty seemed to benefit him or her in some significant way. Did that person's influence change the way you approached similar situations? When dishonest people succeed, how does an honest person reconcile the matter internally?

HUMOR

- Relate a personal story that demonstrates the value of a sense of humor in business. Do you have a sense of humor? How important is humor in your life? Give me an example of humor misused.

- Give me some examples of ways in which you handle stress and tension at work. Does humor play a role? How does it help? When is it appropriate? What special cautions are warranted?

INDEPENDENCE

- Describe the amount of independence that you have in your present job. What do you like about working independently? What do you dislike about it? How important an issue is independence in the job you're seeking?

- Describe the amount of independence that you allow those working for you. Do you allow different levels of independence to workers based on some qualifier? What does it take to qualify? What happens when those you've allowed to function independently abuse the situation?

INITIATIVE

- Give me an example of a time when you took the initiative to lobby for changes in corporate policy or procedure. What were the risks? How did you approach the situation? What did you do to convince others that changes were needed?

- Give me an example from your work experience that demonstrates how your personal initiative helped you move to positions of greater responsibility. Where does your initiative come from?

INNOVATION

- Tell me about the last innovative suggestion you made about the work you do. To whom was it made? What happened as a result of the suggestion? Was your suggestion given a fair hearing?

- Tell me about a time when you took the initiative rather than waiting to be told what to do. What was involved? What were the risks? What did your initiative accomplish?

INTERPERSONAL SKILLS

- Give me some examples of the contributions that you've made to create a team environment. What does it take to create a sense of team? What things are important to maintaining a team spirit? How do you deal with those who simply refuse to be team players?

- From your experience, give me an example of the importance of interpersonal skills to the success of a manager. What things do you say or do that reflect good interpersonal skills? In hiring new employees, what value do you place on finding people with good interpersonal skills? Why?

INQUISITIVENESS

- (Continuum) On a continuum between independently seeking information and depending upon others to provide you with the information you need to do your job, where would you fit? Why?

- Give me an example of a project that you've worked on in which being inquisitive was a real plus. How did it help? What did being inquisitive produce in terms of results?

INTERNET SKILLS

- Give me an example of the way in which you have used the Internet on the job. How did you learn to use the Internet? What applications do you think the Internet has for our business in the future?

JUDGMENT

- Give me an example of a time when your good judgment helped solve a major problem. What was involved?

- Tell me about a time when you used your best judgment in a situation and later found that you were wrong. How did you discover you were wrong? What did you do to rectify the situation? How costly was the error? What did you learn by it?

KNOWLEDGE

- Tell me about a time when your technical or professional knowledge made an important difference. What were the circumstances?

- Describe a time when it became obvious that you possessed a greater knowledge of the technical aspects of your job than your supervisor. How did you make the discovery? How did that alter your relationship with your supervisor? If you knew more, why weren't you the boss?

LEADERSHIP

- Of all the projects you've worked on during the course of your career, which one best exemplifies your leadership skills? How often do you have an opportunity to provide real leadership in your present job? What's the difference between leadership and managership, and which of those two terms best describes your approach to business?

- Recall the first time you were placed in a position of leadership within a company. What did you do right? What could you have done better? In your opinion, what's the most important key to effective leadership?

LISTENING

- Give me an example of a situation in which good listening skills were required of you. How did you develop your listening skills? Why is it important to be a good listener? What are some of the situations in which good listening skills are a must?

- Tell me about a time when you would have made a different decision if you had been practicing better listening techniques. What did you learn from the experience? In what ways have you become a better listener since that time?

LOYALTY

- Recall for me a time when you weren't as loyal to your company as you should have been. What did you do? How did it feel? What should you have done differently?

- Tell me about a time when, because of a subordinate's loyalty to the company, and particularly the department you supervise, a significant piece of work was accomplished. What kinds of things do you do to inspire loyalty?

MANAGEMENT

- Tell me about the most unpopular management decision you've ever made. What steps did you take in evaluating alternatives? How did you gather the facts that you needed? How did you explain your decision to employees? How did you deal with negative reaction?

- Tell me about the things you've done to build morale in the department that you now manage. How important is employee morale? How do you go about "catching" employees doing something right?

MARKETING

- Tell me about a strategic marketing plan that you developed and the result of its implementation. What research was necessary before developing the plan? Who was involved? What changes did the plan make in the way your organization does business?

- Tell me about a recent marketing questionnaire that you developed. What was its purpose? What did you learn? What is your experience with focus groups? What other marketing research tools have you used?

MENTORING

- Tell me about a mentoring situation that you arranged that worked particularly well. Is mentoring a regular part of new employee training? What are the benefits of a good mentoring program? What are the drawbacks?

- Give me an example of someone who failed in spite of having the benefit of a mentor. What went wrong? What could have been done differently? How did that incident change your mentoring program?

MOTIVATION

- Think of a time when things were not going well. How did you keep yourself going? What do you typically do to help motivate yourself? What do you think is the most motivating aspect of your present job? What is there in the job you're pursuing that you would find motivational?

- Tell me about the most significant failure you've experienced as a manager. How did you handle it? How did the failure affect your personal motivation? How did you overcome it? How did the situation affect the motivation of other members of the team? What did you learn by it?

NEGOTIATION

- Give me an example of a particularly difficult negotiation in which you participated. What was involved? Was it a successful negotiation? How so? How often in your present job have you been in the position of negotiator?

- Tell me about a time when you attempted to negotiate something, to no avail. What was involved? What were the problems? What could you have done differently, or better? What is your approach to negotiation?

NURTURING

- Tell me about the last time you found yourself nurturing a customer, client, or employee. What did you hope to ultimately gain? Is time spent in this way well invested? What kinds of activities are included in your nurturing efforts?

- Describe how you train supervisors under you to nurture new employees. What's the payoff?

OBJECTIVITY

- Tell me about an emotionally charged situation in which it was difficult for you to remain objective. Did you remain objective? How did you accomplish it? How did your objectivity help calm the situation or solve the problem?

- Recall a time when you were dealing with a problem at work in which you lost objectivity and made an emotional decision.

What happened? Had you remained more objective, what kind
of decision would you have made? What lessons did you learn
from the situation?

Observation

- Relate a situation from your present job that demonstrates the
  importance of being observant. What do you hope to discover?
  What do you do with the information that you obtain in this
  manner? How did you develop this skill?

- Tell me about your ability to be observant of others. How has
  that ability helped you in your present position? How do you
  think that ability would help you in the job you're seeking?

Open-Mindedness

- (Continuum) On a continuum between favoring established
  methods of doing business and being completely open to new
  ideas, where would you fit?

- Tell me about the last time that a subordinate came to you
  with a new idea. What did the idea involve? How did you
  respond? What do you do to promote an atmosphere of "out-
  of-the-box" thinking among employees reporting to you?
  Was the employee's idea implemented?

Output

- Tell me about a time when your team broke records in terms
  of production quantity. What was involved? Was breaking the
  record a defined objective of the team? How did you keep up
  enthusiasm? What were the most important steps that led to
  success?

- Give me an example of the last time that you intervened in a
  situation involving poor employee productivity. What was

happening? How did you learn of the problem? What did you
do to solve the problem? What could you have done better?

OWNERSHIP

- Describe an incident that demonstrates that those who report
  to you really take ownership of their team and the work they
  accomplish individually and together. How is the attitude of
  ownership instilled? Do those to whom you report take the
  same kind of ownership for their work?

- Tell me about a time when it was difficult to take responsibility for something at work. What was the problem? What did
  taking ownership of the situation mean in practical terms?
  What did you learn from the experience? What did those who
  report to you learn?

PATIENCE

- From your management experience, tell me about a time
  when patience really paid off for you. How patient an individual are you normally? How did you develop your ability
  to be patient? Does patience ever get in the way of progress?

- Tell me about a time when you simply lost your patience and
  demanded that something happen immediately. What were
  the circumstances? What was the reaction to your demand for
  immediate response? What did you learn from the situation?
  When, if ever, should a manager set aside patience for the
  good of the organization?

PERCEPTIVENESS

- From your business experience, tell me about a time when
  your perception helped you in some significant way.

- (Self-appraisal) If I were to ask your references how perceptive they think you are, what would they tell me?

PERSISTENCE

- Relate a scenario in which your persistence really paid off. What was at stake? How did you demonstrate persistence?

- Describe the most difficult sale that you ever made. What were you selling? What was the competition? What did you do by way of planning the sale? What role did persistence play?

PERSUASIVENESS

- (Self-appraisal) How persuasive are you? If I were to ask your present supervisor to comment on your persuasive abilities, what would she tell me? Where did you learn how to be persuasive?

- Sell me the product that you now represent. In terms of sales ranking, where do you stand in relation to other members of your company's sales force?

PLANNING

- Tell me about a time when inadequate planning caused a major mess. What was involved? What role were you playing in the project? What elements of planning were inadequately addressed? What was the result?

- Describe a situation in which you were in charge of planning a major project or event. How did you approach the task? What steps did you take to ensure that an adequate job of planning would be done? When you finished your task of planning, how did you communicate the final product? What difference did your plan make?

POLITENESS

- Tell me about a time when simply being courteous made a major difference. How important is courtesy in your present job? How important do you think it is in the job you're seeking? Why?

- (Self-appraisal) If I were to ask your references about your courtesy to others, what would they tell me?

PRACTICALITY

- Describe a situation that required you to be very practical in the way you approached it. Why did it matter? Why is it important to be practical in business matters?

- Give me an example of a training situation that you offer new employees that emphasizes practicality. Why is that important? What steps do you take to ensure that practicality is part of every training program?

PRECISION

- Give me an example of a time when your ability to be precise made a significant difference in an assigned task or project. How did you develop the skill to be precise? How often are you required to be precise in your present job?

- (Continuum) On a scale between being concerned about precision and being concerned about quantity of work completed, where do you fit?

PRESENTATION

- Give me an example of a recent presentation that you gave. Was it successful? Why do you think so? What did you do to plan the presentation? What elements of the presentation were particularly important? What did the presentation accomplish?

- Describe the elements of a good sales presentation that you recently made. Why are each of these elements important? How many presentations does it take to make a sale? What's the norm for a salesman with your present company?

Process Following

- From your experience in your present job, give me an example of the value of an established process in conducting business. Why is process so important? Should a process be flexible or inflexible? Why?

- Tell me about a primary process that's involved in performing your present job. Are there any parts of the process that could work better? When did you last suggest changes to the process? What was the result?

Production

- Give me an example of a sales situation in which you outproduced other members of your team. How did you do it? How important is it to be a top producer? Why?

- (Continuum) On a continuum between being a thinker and being a producer, where would you fit?

Progressiveness

- Tell me about a time when you recommended a major improvement to your present company's management. What needed fixing? What would your recommendation accomplish?

- Describe a time when someone who reports to you recommended the adoption of a new method or invention to

improve the quality of the work product. What did you do as
a result of the suggestion? Was the suggestion implemented?
Why or why not? What do you do to encourage progressive
thinking among members of your team?

PROJECT MANAGEMENT

- Tell me about a successful project that you've recently man-
  aged. What kind of planning is involved in a major project?
  What is a project milestone? When you assign a project, what
  steps do you take to ensure that the project will be completed
  on time?

- Tell me about a time when a project that you were managing
  began to exceed budget expectations. What steps did you
  take? Whom did you involve? Were you able to correct the
  problem?

PROSPECTING

- Give me an example of the way in which you go about finding new customers. Is it effective? On average, how many
  prospects does it take to produce one sale?

- Tell me about the kind of people you normally like to sell to.
  Why this particular group? Have you always preferred this
  kind of buyer? What kind of person do you least like to sell
  to? Why?

PUBLIC RELATIONS

- Tell me about a recent work experience that demonstrates
  your commitment to public relations. How important is public
  relations to your present firm? From your experience, what
  are the most important factors for good public relations?

- Relate a situation in which the issue of public relations was not given the consideration that it deserved. What was the impact? What did you learn from the situation?

Punctuality

- Tell me about a situation at work in which very few seem to be concerned about promptness. Are you prompt? Why is that important to you? What do you do to ensure your own promptness?

- Tell me how you encourage the promptness of others when they're working on projects that you've assigned them. What happens when someone fails to be prompt?

Quality

- Tell me about a time when work performed by those reporting to you did not meet your expectations for quality. What was happening? How did you discover the problem? What steps did you take to correct the situation?

- Describe a situation that demonstrates your commitment to customer satisfaction. How do you inspire that same commitment in others? Why is quality and customer satisfaction important to your business?

Quota Making

- Tell me about the last time that your monthly sales were below expectations (or quota). What happened to produce the problem? What did you do to get back on track?

- Recall a time when your sales team was functioning below expectations. What did you do to turn the situation around?

RELIABILITY

- (Self-appraisal) If I were to ask your references to tell me how reliable of an employee you are, what would they say?

- Recall a time when you had to deal with a subordinate over the issue of reliability. What was happening? How did you approach the issue? What kind of plan did you mutually develop that addressed the issue of becoming more reliable?

REPORT WRITING

- Tell me about the last major report that you wrote. What did you like least about it? How do you prepare to write a major report? What are the important elements of a good report? What steps do you take to ensure accuracy and readability?

- How important is report writing for those who presently report to you? Tell me about a situation that demonstrates the need for good report-writing skills. What report-writing assistance do you offer those who report to you?

REPRIMANDING

- Tell me about the last time that you had to formally reprimand a subordinate. What prompted the reprimand? How did you proceed? What was the result of the reprimand?

- Give me a few examples of the kinds of work performance issues that have prompted you to formally reprimand a subordinate. What kinds of corrective action did you attempt before the formal reprimand? In your experience, have formal reprimands been helpful in correcting employee misconduct? Does the threat of reprimands prevent misconduct?

RESEARCHING

- Describe your last major research project. How many people were involved? What was the objective of the project? How did you organize the project? How were results compiled?

- Tell me about a time when your instincts were proven wrong by research data. What was involved? How did you confirm the accuracy of data? How did you present your findings?

RISK TAKING

- Tell me about the last time you took a major risk and it paid off. What was at stake? What made you think that taking the risk was the right thing to do? In practical terms, what would have happened had you been wrong?

- Tell me about risks that those who report to you may occasionally take. What latitude do you provide subordinates who are assigned a specific task or project? How do you react when a subordinate takes a risk and fails?

SELLING

- Tell me what you dislike most about selling. How have you tried to overcome this dislike? What do you do to make it tolerable? How has this dislike affected your ability to sell?

- Tell me about a very special award that you've won for selling? What did it take to earn the award? Where was it given? How difficult was it to earn? What awards do you hope to win in the future?

SENSITIVITY

- Give me an example of a time at work when real sensitivity was required of you. Did you meet the challenge? Do others view you as a sensitive person? How do you know?

- (Contrary evidence) How important is it for a manager to be sensitive to the needs of his subordinates? Tell me about a time when you weren't as sensitive as you should have been. What happened as a result? What did you learn? How did you learn to identify situations that require greater sensitivity?

Speaking

- Tell me about an occasion in which you spoke before a large group of people. How did you prepare? What message did you convey? How did you organize your speech? What did you like about it? What could you have done better?

- Describe the most significant speech that you've ever heard. Who was speaking? What was there about it that made an impression on you? Do you enjoy public speaking? What kinds of speeches do you least enjoy?

Strategizing

- Tell me about a time when it was necessary for you to develop a strategy to accomplish a specific work objective. What was the objective? What were the steps necessary to reach the objective? What was the strategy that you utilized to get there?

- Tell me about a situation that would have turned out differently had more time been taken to strategize. Why wasn't it done? What did you learn from the situation?

Stress Management

- Tell me about the most stressful job you've ever held. What made it stressful? How did you cope?

- Give me an example of the kinds of stressors that are involved in your present job. What do you do to overcome them?

SUPPORTIVENESS

- From whom do you derive most of your support in your present job? Give me an example of what that person says and does to communicate support. How important is it to have the support of others?

- Give me a few examples of how you support those who report to you. How important is this kind of support? How do you know that your support efforts are worthwhile?

TEAM BUILDING

- (Contrary evidence) How important is developing a sense of teamwork among those working in your department? Tell me about a time when you attempted to use a management style that did not involve team building.

- Tell me about the team that you supervise now. What makes it a team? What are the team's strengths and weaknesses? What objectives have you met as a team? How do you foster a team spirit?

TECHNICAL SKILLS

- Describe what you did through the past year to expand your technical knowledge. How do you feel about continuing technical training? Do you do things other than attending formal training to keep yourself current?

- Tell me, in the hiring process, how you go about determining whether a candidate is technically competent. As a manager, what kinds of ongoing technical training do you require?

TERMINATION

- Tell me about the last time you terminated an employee. What led up to the termination? How did you approach the situation? How long had you been counseling this particular employee? Who made the final decision to terminate? Did you concur? Was the employee given an opportunity to resign? How will you handle future requests for information about the employee?

- Tell me about the last time you were fired from a job. What kind of job was involved? What went wrong? Were you dealt with in a fair and equitable manner? What did the situation teach you?

TRAINING

- Tell me about the kind of mandatory training that you feel should be provided to new employees coming into your department. How does that differ from what they are actually being offered?

- Tell me about the last time that you advocated for better training. To whom did you make your case? What were the reasons you gave for your position? How did you suggest better training could be accomplished? What was the result?

WINNING

- Tell me about the last time you and your team won something significant. How did it feel? Did winning just happen, or was it planned? What did you do to make it happen? What effect did winning have on the team and its attitude toward future projects?

- Is it fair to say that your experience has taught you a number of winning techniques, philosophies, and strategies? Tell me about a few of them that you would bring with you if you were given the position with our company.

Appendix B

Interview Evaluation Summary

Name of candidate: _____

Position: _____

Interviewer: _____

Date: _____

Candidate summary (prepared by hiring manager): _____

Mandatory Success Factor	Rating	Weight	Total Points

TOTAL SCORE

Rating = 1 to 5 (highest)

Weight = Prioritized mandatory success factors (Example: Given 10 prioritized factors, factor 1 would have a weight of 10, factor 2 would have a weight of 9, and so on.)

Appendix C
Glossary

active listening   An interview technique, with origins in the field of psychotherapy, that helps assure candidates that the interviewer is listening to them intently. Active listening involves encouraging candidates to talk openly and freely by often reflecting back to them the meaning of their communication, both verbal and nonverbal, in ways that promote further exploration and awareness.

disclosure agreements   Legally binding instruments between an employer and an employee who is leaving the organization. The agreement purposely limits what can later be disclosed to prospective employers.

green flags   Specific items in the resumé of an applicant that clearly demonstrate positive achievement, especially in areas involving identified mandatory success factors.

hypothetical   Situations that are imaginary. Hypothetical interview questions attempt to discover how a candidate would act if a certain situation were to occur; both the question and the response are purely conjecture.

introspective investigation   The process by which an organization thoroughly examines a position to be filled. The goal of introspective investigation is to identify essential competencies, skills, and abilities that are required for successful performance.

intuitive listening   Being sensitive to what *is* said and what *is not* said. It is the message conveyed by a hesitation, a reluctance to discuss a matter, or the obvious desire to change the subject.

mandatory success factors   Those specific competencies and skills that have been identified to be absolutely essential to successful job performance. Mandatory success factors are determined through a process of introspective investigation and provide a profile of the job as well as the ideal candidate.

negligence   The failure to exercise a reasonable amount of care, which results in injury or damage to another.

open behavioral questions   Questions that cannot be answered with a simple "yes" or "no." They require a candidate to discuss at length a specific incident from the past that required a working knowledge of specific skills.

postoffer stage   The stage of the selection process when a conditional offer of employment has been extended to an applicant. Conditional offers are made when present employers have yet to be contacted, or when the offer is subject to the applicant passing a medical examination.

preoffer stage   The stage of the selection process before an employer extends a conditional offer of employment to a candidate.

probe   A question or request that seeks specific information, clarification, or confirmation from a candidate being interviewed. Probes may be open or closed, depending on the intended purpose.

reasonable accommodation   The legal requirement that employers find ways to provide equal opportunity to protected classes of employees, including those with disabilities and those who require special accommodations for religious practices. It may even include the possibility of transferring the employee to another job if that becomes necessary to accommodate the religious needs of the employee.

red flags   Those factors in a resumé that indicate danger and require further exploration with the applicant, or that support rejection of the resumé from further consideration.

reliability   Refers to the consistency of scores and measurement that is free of error.

short list   A list of a few select candidates who have achieved the highest scores in an initial interview and have been chosen for further consideration.

soft measurements   Tests and inventories based mostly on self-reporting beliefs and feelings, or past behavior. There are no right or wrong answers.

technospeak   Refers to words and phrases that are particularly in vogue within special segments of society but that are not generally understood or recognized by outsiders.

validity   Refers to the extent that a given test actually measures what it is designed to measure.

INDEX

Q